More than **200,000** student reviews on nearly **7,000** schools!

SEE IT ALL ON COLLEGEPROWLER.COM!

This book only offers a glimpse at our extensive coverage of one school out of thousands across the country. Visit *collegeprowler.com* to view our full library of content for FREE! Our site boasts thousands of photos and videos, interactive search tools, more reviews, and expanded content on nearly 7,000 schools.

CONNECT WITH SCHOOLS
Connect with the schools you are most interested in and discover new schools that match your interests.

FIND SCHOLARSHIPS
We give away $2,000 each month and offer personalized matches from a database of more than 3.2 million other scholarships!

SELECT A MAJOR
We have information on every major in the country to help you choose your degree and plan your career.

USE OUR TOOLS TO HELP YOU CHOOSE
Compare schools side-by-side, estimate your chances of admission, and get personalized school recommendations.

To get started, visit <u>collegeprowler.com/register</u>

WWW.COLLEGEPROWLER.COM

The Big Book of Colleges

Choosing the perfect school can be an overwhelming challenge. Luckily, our *Big Book of Colleges* makes that task a little less daunting. We've packed it with overviews of our full library of single-school guides—more than 400 of the nation's top schools—giving you some much-needed perspective on your search.

BIG BOOK OF COLLEGES '12
Paperback 7.75" X 10", 900+ pages
$29.95 Retail
ISBN: 978-1-4274-0326-1

*To order your copy,
visit collegeprowler.com/store*

Washington & Lee University

Lexington, VA

Written by Zachary John Barbieri, Jeremiah McWilliams

Edited by the College Prowler Team

ISBN # 978-1-4274-0693-4

©Copyright 2011 College Prowler

All Rights Reserved
Printed in the U.S.A.
www.collegeprowler.com

Last updated: 3/24/2011

College Prowler®
5001 Baum Blvd.
Suite 750
Pittsburgh, PA 15213

Phone: (800) 290-2682
Fax: (800) 772-4972
E-Mail: info@collegeprowler.com
Web: www.collegeprowler.com

©Copyright 2011 College Prowler.

All rights reserved. No part of this work may be reproduced or transmitted in any form or by any means, including but not limited to, photocopy, recording, or any information storage and retrieval systems, without the express written permission of College Prowler®.

College Prowler® is not sponsored by, affiliated with, or approved by Washington & Lee University in any way.

College Prowler® strives faithfully to record its sources. As the reader understands, opinions, impressions, and experiences are necessarily personal and unique. Accordingly, there are, and can be, no guarantees of future satisfaction extended to the reader.

How this all started...

When I was trying to find the perfect college, I used every resource that was available to me. I went online to visit school Web sites; I talked with my high school guidance counselor; I read book after book; I hired a private counselor. Sure, this was all very helpful, but nothing really told me what life was like at the schools I cared about. These sources weren't giving me enough information to be totally confident in my decision.

In all my research, there were only two ways to get the information I wanted.

The first was to physically visit the campuses and see if things were really how the brochures described them, but this was quite expensive and not always feasible. The second involved a missing ingredient: the students. Actually talking to a few students at those schools gave me a taste of the information that I needed so badly. The problem was that I wanted more but didn't have access to enough people.

In the end, I weighed my options and decided on a school that felt right and had a great academic reputation, but truth be told, the choice was still very much a crapshoot. I had done as much research as any other student, but was I 100 percent positive that I had picked the school of my dreams?

Absolutely not.

My dream in creating College Prowler was to build a resource that people can use with confidence. My own college search experience taught me the importance of gaining true insider insight; that's why the majority of this guide is composed of quotes from actual students. After all, shouldn't you hear about a school from the people who know it best?

I hope you enjoy reading this book as much as we've enjoyed putting it together. Tell me what you think when you get a chance. I'd love to hear your college selection stories.

Luke Skurman
CEO and Co-Founder
luke@collegeprowler.com

Welcome to College Prowler®

When we created College Prowler, we felt it was critical that our content was unbiased and unaffiliated with any college or university. We think it's important that our readers get honest information and a realistic impression of the student opinions on any campus—that's why if any aspect of a particular school is terrible, we (unlike a campus brochure) intend to publish it. While we do keep an eye out for the occasional extremist—the cheerleader or the cynic—we take pride in letting the students tell it like it is. We strive to create a book that's as representative as possible of each particular campus. Our books cover both the good and the bad, and whether the survey responses point to recurring trends or a variation in opinion, these sentiments are directly and proportionally expressed through our guides.

College Prowler guidebooks are in the hands of students throughout the entire process of their creation. Because you can't make student-written guides without the students, we have students at each campus who help write, randomly survey their peers, edit, layout, and perform accuracy checks on every book that we publish. From the very beginning, student writers gather the most up-to-date stats, facts, and inside information on their colleges. They fill each section with student quotes and summarize the findings in editorial reviews. In addition, each school receives a collection of letter grades (A through F) that reflect student opinion and help to represent contentment or satisfaction for each of our 20 specific categories. Just as in grade school, the higher the mark the more content or more satisfied the students are with the particular category.

Each book is the result of endless student contributions, hundreds of pages of research and writing, and countless hours of hard work. All of this has led to the creation of a student information network that stretches across the nation to every school that we cover. It's no easy accomplishment, but it's the reason that our guides are such a great resource.

When reading our books and looking at our grades, keep in mind that every college is different and that the students who make up each school are not uniform—as a result, it is important to assess schools on a case-by-case basis. Because it's impossible to summarize an entire school with a single number or description, each book provides a dialogue, not a decision, that's made up of 20 different topics and hundreds of student quotes. In the end, we hope that this guide will serve as a valuable tool in your college selection process. Enjoy!

The College Prowler Team

WASHINGTON & LEE UNIVERSITY
Table of Contents

By the Numbers.................. **1**

Academics **4**

Local Atmosphere **11**

Health & Safety.................. **17**

Computers......................... **23**

Facilities............................ **29**

Campus Dining.................. **35**

Off-Campus Dining **42**

Campus Housing **51**

Off-Campus Housing.......... **59**

Diversity............................ **63**

Guys & Girls....................... **70**

Athletics............................ **75**

Nightlife............................ **83**

Greek Life **89**

Drug Scene........................ **95**

Campus Strictness **100**

Parking............................ **105**

Transportation **111**

Weather **116**

Report Card Summary ... **120**

Overall Experience **121**

The Inside Scoop............ **125**

Jobs & Internships.......... **131**

Alumni & Post-Grads **135**

Student Organizations.... **138**

The Best **141**

The Worst **142**

Visiting............................ **143**

Words to Know **145**

By the Numbers

School Contact

Washington & Lee University
204 West Washington Street
Lexington, VA 24450

Control:
Private Non-Profit

Academic Calendar:
Semester

Religious Affiliation:
None

Founded:
1749

Web Site:
www.wlu.edu

Main Phone:
(540) 458-8400

Student Body

Full-Time Undergraduates:
1,760

Part-Time Undergraduates:
2

Total Male Undergraduates:
894

Total Female Undergraduates:
882

Admissions

Acceptance Rate:
19%

Total Applicants:
6,222

Total Acceptances:
1,181

Freshman Enrollment:
472

Yield (% of admitted students who enroll):
40%

Applicants Placed on Waiting List:
872

Applicants Accepting a Place on Waiting List:
282

Students Enrolled from Waiting List:
31

Transfer Applications Received:
111

Transfer Applications Accepted:
17

Transfer Students Enrolled:
10

Transfer Application Acceptance Rate:
15%

SAT I or ACT Required?
Either

SAT I Range (25th–75th Percentile):
1970–2200

SAT I Verbal Range (25th–75th Percentile):
660–740

SAT I Math Range (25th–75th Percentile):
660–730

SAT I Writing Range (25th–75th Percentile):
650–730

ACT Composite Range (25th–75th Percentile):
29–32

ACT English Range (25th–75th Percentile):
30–34

ACT Math Range (25th–75th Percentile):
28–32

ACT Writing Range (25th–75th Percentile):
29–33

Top 10% of High School Class:
84%

Application Fee:
$50

Common Application Accepted?
Yes

Admissions Phone:
(540) 458-8710

Admissions E-Mail:
admissions@wlu.edu

Admissions Web Site:
admissions.wlu.edu

Regular Decision Deadline:
January 15

Regular Decision Notification:
April 1

Must-Reply-By Date:
May 1

Financial Information

Out-of-State Tuition:
$38,877

Room and Board:
$8,755

Books and Supplies:
$1,650

Average Amount of Federal Grant Aid:
$5,425

Percentage of Students Who Received Federal Grant Aid:
4%

Average Amount of Institution Grant Aid:
$25,373

Percentage of Students Who Received Institution Grant Aid:
41%

Average Amount of State Grant Aid:
$2,612

Percentage of Students Who Received State Grant Aid:
17%

Average Amount of Student Loans:
$5,407

Percentage of Students Who Received Student Loans:
28%

Total Need-Based Package:
$30,933

Percentage of Students Who Received Any Aid:
66%

Financial Aid Forms Deadline:
February 1

Financial Aid Phone:
(540) 458-8717

Financial Aid E-Mail:
financialaid@wlu.edu

Financial Aid Web Site:
www.wlu.edu/x437.xml

Academics

The Lowdown On...
Academics

Degrees Awarded
Bachelor's degree
Master's degree

Most Popular Majors
Business Administration and Management
Economics and Econometrics
Law
Political Science and Government, General

Majors Offered
Arts
Biological Sciences
Business
Communications
Computer and Sciences
Engineering
Environmental Sciences
Languages and Literature
Law
Mathematics & Statistics
Philosophy and Religion
Physical Sciences

Psychology & Counseling
Social Sciences & Liberal Arts
Social Services

Undergraduate Schools/Divisions
The College
The Williams School of Commerce, Economics, and Politics

Full-Time Instructional Faculty
272

Part-Time Instructional Faculty
71

Faculty with Terminal Degree
96%

Average Faculty Salary
$95,710

Student-Faculty Ratio
7:1

Class Sizes
Fewer than 20 Students: 68%
20 to 49 Students: 31%
50 or More Students: 1%

Full-Time Retention Rate
94%

Graduation Rate
89%

Remedial Services?
No

Academic/Career Counseling?
Yes

Instructional Programs
Occupational: No
Academic: Yes
Continuing Professional: No
Recreational/Avocational: No
Adult Basic Remedial: No
Secondary (High School): No

Special Credit Opportunities
Advanced Placement (AP) Credits: Yes
Dual Credit: Yes
Life Experience Credits: No

Special Study Options
Study abroad
Teacher certification (below the postsecondary level)

Best Places to Study
The Commons living room
Fraternity/sorority common room
Friend's room
Journalism School computer lab
Leyburn Library
Science Library
Williams School reading room

Did You Know?

W&L is the ninth-oldest college in the country; it traces its founding to 1749 (it started as Augusta Academy). Come back in 2049 for the opening of the mysterious time capsule.

Washington and Lee's honor system is legendary. W&L is one of a handful of universities with honor systems run entirely by students. Cases involving plagiarism, lying, theft, and sometimes harassment are brought up before the elected, all-student Executive Committee. So behave—the only punishment for a violation is withdrawal from the school. Professors say the Honor Code gives them confidence in students, who can schedule their own exams and sometimes take them home overnight. Students say it lets them leave valuables around campus without fear.

Where in the world are W&L students? Well, about 45 percent of the class of 2004 went abroad to study during their time at the University. Students can go all over the world, from Scotland to Spain, Japan, and Brazil.

Students can get credit for working in the U.S. Senate, CBS News, or the White House in the Washington Term Program, organized through the politics department. Students spend the six-week spring term in Washington DC and in past semesters have schmoozed with the likes of Dick Cheney and Congressman Jim Davis.

Students Speak Out On...
Academics

Q Availability :
Washington and Lee professors are always available for students. There is practically no need to schedule an appointment to meet them, and they are all more than delighted to meet with the students even outside their office hours.

Q Professors are extremely approachable—they love to interact with students. I hadn't even been here a week before I had been invited to a professor's house for dinner. Since W&L expects professors to spend a lot of time teaching (and not quite as much time doing research), the school attracts professors who prize prof-student interaction.

Q Classes tend to be small and discussion-based. Freshmen can anticipate a lot of choice in their class selections, and professors and advisors who are eager to help them navigate individual classes and general education requirements. As you get into your major, you tend to know more and more of your fellow majors. Professors frequently consult upperclassman majors when they plan courses or consider changing teaching strategies. All professors administer and consult end-of-course evaluations (some even do midterm evaluations) to find ways of better teaching their students.

Q My professors are very friendly, which is wonderful and a burden at the same time—but a good burden. You feel more pressure to do well in his or her class since you do not want to disappoint your friend.

Q Every teacher I've had (and I'm a senior) has been extremely accessible. All have set office hours, but they also have no problem if you drop in on them unannounced to ask a question or just chat.

Q In the past week, I've slept on the science floor instead of going home on one night, and on another day, I studied there from 11 in the morning to midnight for a test—and you question how hard the science department is?

Q Registration is easy! The University Registrar is always on top of things: the online pre-registration and registration systems work wonderfully. Information about class size and class availability is easily accessible. Besides, in both of my majors, a student who has declared the major is never denied a spot in a class.

Q Freshmen can expect to be challenged. And they need to get over the fact that they were 4.0 students in high school, because the reality is that they may never see that number again, no matter how hard they try.

The College Prowler Take On...
Academics

Make no mistake: academic work at Washington and Lee is intense. Professors expect a lot of effort and take great pride in not inflating grades. If you get an A+ here, cherish it, because it might be the only one you'll see. On the positive side, students build personal relationships with the faculty, and can rely on them for help whenever they hit a rough spot. Professors keep ample office hours and have students over for some down-home cooking. Certain old-school history profs have also been known to share a few drinks with their pupils at the Palms, but that's another story. Also, classes at Washington and Lee are taught exclusively by professors—no teaching assistants allowed.

At Washington and Lee, students are required to take a broad selection of classes—general education credits, or "gen eds"—outside of their majors. This kind of work typically makes up one-third of the courseload. Some of W&L's coolest programs are interdisciplinary—the courses cut across the usual majors and create hybrid offerings that attract all kinds of students. The Shepherd Program for Poverty combines economics, politics, and philosophy in academic study, and volunteer work helps students get their hands dirty with real-world problems. Students can dip into economics, literature, and science in the environmental studies program, or peruse philosophy, music, and art in the medieval and renaissance studies major. There is even a class on superheroes here for the comic book lover. Needless to say, Washington and Lee has a course offering for any and all interests students could possibly have.

The College Prowler® Grade on
Academics: A

A high Academics grade generally indicates that professors are knowledgeable, accessible, and genuinely interested in their students' welfare. Other determining factors include class size, how well professors communicate, and whether or not classes are engaging.

Local Atmosphere

The Lowdown On...
Local Atmosphere

City, State
Lexington, VA

Distances to Nearest Major Cities
Richmond – VA – 2 hours, 30 minutes
Roanoke – VA – 1 hour
Washington – D.C. – 3 hours

Points of Interest
Carriage tours of Lexington
George C. Marshall Museum at the Virginia Military Institute
Lee Chapel and Museum
Natural Bridge and Caverns
Rockbridge Vineyard
The Stonewall Jackson House
The Theatre at Lime Kiln
The Virginia Horse Center

Shopping Centers
Tanglewood Mall
Valley Mall
Valley View Mall

Major Sports Teams
None

Movie Theaters
Hull's Drive-In
2367 N Lee Hwy.
Lexington
(540) 463-2621

State Theatre
12 E Nelson St.
Lexington
(540) 463-3424

Did You Know?

5 Fun Facts about Lexington:

• "The shot heard 'round the world"—the town of Lexington was established in 1778, and named in honor of the Battle of Lexington, Massachusetts between ye olde colonials and redcoats.

• Robert E. Lee and Thomas "Stonewall" Jackson both lived here. Their houses are in downtown Lexington.

• Sam Houston was born in a log cabin just north of Lexington in 1793.

• Hollywood? Who needs Hollywood? Scenes for Gods and Generals (2003; Robert Duvall), Sommersby (1993; Richard Gere, Jodie Foster), and War of the Worlds (2005; Stephen Spielberg, Tom Cruise) were filmed in and around Lexington. Washington and Lee's front lawn and the barracks at VMI the (Virginia Military Institute) make early appearances in Gods and Generals.

• The National Park Service calls Washington and Lee's front campus "one of the nation's most dignified and beautiful campuses."

Students Speak Out On...
Local Atmosphere

Q There are lots of things to do outdoors, like hiking, kayaking, biking, running, and camping. We have House Mountain nearby, the New River is a couple of hours away in a car (great white water rafting and kayaking), and Natural Bridge is a 20-minute drive. Aside from that, there are beautiful little towns nearby like Staunton and Charlottesville that are fun to walk around if you want to get off campus for a day.

Q If you like outdoor activities, Lexington is the place for you. There are so many awesome national parks, hiking trails, and fly-fishing rivers. Also, the Outing Club is an unbelievable resource—a one-time $30 registration fee gives you access to fly-fishing equipment, hiking equipment, canoes, and kayaks.

Q The town can be a little stifling at times, just in terms of size, but the atmosphere is good. The College has a good relationship with the surrounding city and the Virginia Military Institute. In a town this size, you are bound to run into friends and professors everywhere you go, from the grocery store to local shops. Sometimes it seems as if the town is an extension of the school.

Q As a W&L freshman orientation T-shirt once said, 'Wal-Mart is like Disneyworld, a magical kingdom.' Wal-Mart is the W&L version of Mecca. It's close and a common destination. Even if you don't have a car, you can usually find someone who is going to Wal-Mart anyway and will be willing to drive.

Q Lexington is a very safe place. I have walked alone on the streets at 2 a.m. in the morning several times. I haven't heard of any major criminal acts in the area over the past three years that I have been here. When you come here, though, use your common sense—you are most likely to get away with it if you don't, but you never know when something weird is going to happen.

Q I like the small town atmosphere, particularly being nestled among the trees and along the little creek. If you are a big-city person, then it might take some getting used to. The orchestra concerts, together with plays, choir concerts, and movies in the school theater, provide other opportunities for entertainment.

Q The Lexington area is one of the most beautiful places I've ever been. The population is rural, but the town is charming, old, and full of intrigue. Everything in town is basically within walking distance, although a car is necessary to get to places like Wal-Mart. The outdoors are definitely a plus in the area—there is a river hotspot about a half an hour from town where you can go tubing, swimming, and sunbathing. And there are plenty of places to hike—we're in the Shenandoah Valley, after all.

Q I wouldn't exactly call Lexington a student-friendly atmosphere, seeing as how everything closes by 7 p.m. and nothing's open on Sundays, but I guess that's why we have fraternities.

The College Prowler Take On...
Local Atmosphere

W&L is nestled in historic Lexington, deep in the heart of Virginia's Shenandoah Valley, This is definitely a small town, rich in heritage and boasting panoramic views of the valley and mountains—some of Virginia's most stunning natural surroundings, History is palpable here—you can catch a horse-drawn carriage tour and see the former homes of "Stonewall" Jackson and Robert E, Lee, The University's main lawn, with massive white columns fronting the line of academic buildings, served as the backdrop for a scene in Gods and Generals,

But there are things to do in the present if the 1860s seem a little distant, Students can hike miles of scenic trails, go tubing down the Maury River, bowl their hearts out, and work on their tan at Goshen Pass, to name a few, Lexington even has its own natural wonder, Natural Bridge, But many students complain that, beyond the bubble of W&L, Lexington and the surrounding area offer little to keep them amused and engaged, Unfortunately, there isn't much interaction with the one other college in town, the Virginia Military Institute (VMI) which is right next door, but worlds away, The drill instructors keep the cadets, known as "Veemies," pretty much under lock and key for their four years in Lexington, so W&L students see very little of the uniformed neighbors, except during Sunday church services or when they jog through campus,

Overall, Lexington is what the students decide to make of it, Some students sit around and complain while others get more involved with Intramural Sports, the outing club, or just relax in their much-coveted free time, For those who cannot live without a mall or big club scene, Roanoke is only an hour away, and it is a pretty decent city... For the rest of this editorial, visit collegeprowler.com.

The College Prowler® Grade on
Local Atmosphere: C-

A high Local Atmosphere grade indicates that the area surrounding campus is safe and scenic. Other factors include nearby attractions, proximity to other schools, and the town's attitude toward students.

Health & Safety

The Lowdown On...
Health & Safety

Security Office
Public Safety Office
(540) 458-8999
www.wlu.edu/x30129.xml

Safety Services
24-hour patrols
Emergency management plans
Emergency phones
Safety escorts
Self-defense PE class (for ladies only)
Traveler safe ride program

Crimes on Campus
Aggravated Assault: 0
Arson: 0
Burglary: 13
Murder/Manslaughter: 0
Robbery: 0
Sex Offenses: 0
Vehicle Theft: 0

Health Center
Student Health Center
Davis Residence Hall, lower level

(540) 458-8401
www.wlu.edu/x7884.xml
Daily 24 hours

Health Services
Allergy shots
Emergency contraceptives
HIV/STD testing
Immunizations
Laboratory
Physician appointments
Referrals
Sexual health
Travel health
Women's health

Day Care Services?
No

Did You Know?

The Infirmary has 10 beds for students who need some supervision but aren't sick enough for the hospital. They're comfy.

Information about all visits to the Health Center/Infirmary is confidential, except when the law or regulations require disclosure.

W&L's security staff has 150 years of combined experience in the art of kicking butt and taking names.

Washington and Lee mans its own on-campus security staff, who are responsible for on-campus enforcement of laws and University regulations. Meanwhile, three police jurisdictions overlap outside of town: County Sheriff's Deptartment, Lexington Police Deptartment, and the Virginia State Police.

Students Speak Out On...
Health & Safety

Q As Safe as It Gets
The honor system assures complete campus safety. Thefts and petty crime rarely occur on campus and even in town. People always leave their doors unlocked - and even open - and their valuables lying around without fear. You can walk around at any time and will not have to call for an escort or friend to go with you.

Q
The police are pretty strict and are looking to give W&L students tickets; students learn quickly to drive the speed limit through VMI and to never walk outside a party where cops have congregated unless you are walking to the Traveler vans.

Q
The cops probably spend more time giving out noise violations and parking tickets than actually making Lexington safer.

Q
Whether campus security guards are strict or lenient depends on the relationship you develop with them. If you're polite, make conversation, and get to know them, they'll usually give you a hand. But if you're rude, and enjoy blatantly breaking the rules and acting like a moron, they'll come down and be as strict as they need to be.

Q
I only lock my dorm room when I'm going to be away from campus for an extended period of time. While I'm around, I keep my door open, even if I go to class or to get lunch. The Honor Code really does result in a safer campus and a great deal of trust between students.

Q I have had better luck calling my sober friends or finding a random sober person at a party than getting Traveler to pay attention to me. The drivers are usually pretty polite, but not necessarily punctual.

Q Security is amazing. The campus is safe, so our security team is here to make sure that we feel safe. We have blue-light phones, as well as available escort service. Members of campus security are friendly and dedicated to their jobs. Campus security will have your car towed, but they will also drive you to the impound lot to re-claim it. The Lexington police handle off-campus incidents. For the most part, they are consistent and fair and don't seem to have an axe to grind when it comes to W&L students.

Q I feel like Lexington's a bubble, and because of our Honor Code, nothing bad can happen—I'm sure I'm being naïve, but I have no reason to think otherwise.

The College Prowler Take On...
Health & Safety

It's elementary, my dear Watson. The students feel remarkably safe at Washington and Lee. Lexington is a sleepy little town at heart, an insulated cocoon with a very low rate of reported violent crime. Partly because of the one-strike Honor Code, students feel free to trust each other with their property. That trust seems to be justified nearly all of the time. Most freshmen don't lock the doors to their dorm rooms, and some upperclassmen keep the habit even after they move into town. In days of yore, students could leave their laptops, purses, or wallets in full view in the library for days on end, and find them undisturbed when they came back—or so the story goes. Today, it's probably not smart to take those chances. Laptops and books have been stolen on campus within the past few years, but the computer thefts (and probably the book heist) were done by non-students. Security guards are not exactly omnipresent on campus, but they respond quickly to calls, and their relations with students tend to be friendly. They can help students with a variety of problems, like pumping up a run-down car battery or opening up a locked door.

The results of a nationwide survey of students were recently released to the student media. It seemed to show that a significant number of cases of unwanted sexual touching and attempted rape go unreported at W&L. The University is making great strides to bring this problem to the forefront and address all of the outreach groups set up for students in such a situation.

The College Prowler® Grade on
Health & Safety: A

A high grade in Health & Safety means that students generally feel safe, campus police are visible, blue-light phones and escort services are readily available, and safety precautions are not overly necessary.

Computers

The Lowdown On...
Computers

Wireless Access
Yes: Almost everywhere on campus---classrooms, commons, fraternities and sororities, the library, residence halls

24-Hour Labs?
Yes: Huntley Hall (C-School), Reid Hall (J-School), Gaines Hall, Newcomb Hall, Robinson Hall, Leyburn Library (1st floor and reference area), Commons, Science Building (Science Library, Howe Hall, Parmly Hall).

Charged to Print?
Yes: 10 cents for black and white, 35 cents for color

Special Software & Hardware Discounts
Discounted software and hardware is available through Information Technology Services at www.wlu.edu/x15930.xml.

Did You Know?

Spam filters and ad-killers can be downloaded directly from W&L's computing site: http://computing.wlu.edu/howto. Hallelujah!

The Leyburn Library was just given a $2.5 million facelift to provide much more productive study space on the first floor. In this space, there are now more than 15 computers provided for students 24 hours a day.

In the journalism school, computers come complete with high-wattage speakers and DVD drives. Students can keep one eye on Sportscenter or The O.C., courtesy of a cable television in the lab.

Students Speak Out On...
Computers

Q You Can Always Find One
Sometimes the labs get crowded, but there are enough you can find one that's empty. WiFi covers the entire campus and there's an extensive remote access setup. Either way, you'll be able to use what you need to.

Q We have wireless inside almost all the major academic buildings and the University Commons. It's fabulous and so helpful. I love bringing my laptop from home and knowing I can work almost anywhere. My wireless card for my off-campus house is the brand W&L recommends, and it's worked out great.

Q I didn't have a computer during my first two years in college, and I didn't feel like I needed one. But that was because the dorms I lived in were pretty close to the University's computer labs. But now that I live a little bit farther away (still walking distance) and have my computer, I feel that I cannot live without it.

Q If network administration staff detect a large amount of traffic to or from your computer due to a P2P file sharing program, your computer is disconnected from the network until the software is removed.

Q At this point, wireless registration at Washington and Lee really couldn't be simpler. Just fill in the Web form with the appropriate info for your wireless card, follow the instructions, and it'll be configured. Wait 30 minutes or so, and the school's network will have processed your registration. Presto, you're good to go!

Q The policy on peer-to-peer file-sharing at Washington and Lee is pretty strict. KaZaA and Morpheus are blocked—at least on the most common ports. Bittorrent is also restricted, and this is really more frustrating than losing some of the other P2P clients, since Bittorrent occassionally has legitimate uses as opposed to downloading copyrighted music and video.

Q The University has a campus wireless network, which covers most of the campus. This clearly makes having a personal laptop an advantage because you are able to walk around campus with it. The wireless network also covers all fraternity and sorority houses.

Q Absolutely bring your own computer. I'd say the vast majority of students bring their own—whether a desk system or a laptop. You'll want to be able to keep an eye on your e-mail from your room and do research on nights when going to a computer lab just doesn't seem too appealing.

The College Prowler Take On...
Computers

Washington and Lee is well stocked with computers that students can use. Some computer labs are well kept secrets: only the chosen few venture into the cold, dusty attic of Newcomb Hall. Others are favorite hangouts; the Commerce School labs are excellent places to find someone to share notes on the accounting test or to put a PowerPoint presentation together. But the C-School labs are notoriously crowded. A better bet is the Reid Hall combination newsroom and computer lab. The intranet allows students to save their work at any location on campus, and then access it at any other computer. There is a generous storage limit, equal to about three years of heavy-duty paper-writing and file-saving. The wireless network works extremely well and is provided across the entire campus, including all student housing.

A free computer can usually be found in any computer lab on campus, although things get very packed during and immediately before finals week. The library recently started renting out brand-new laptops for four hours at a stretch—very cool. Most students bring their own computers, but this is not completely necessary unless they value that extra assurance. University Computing is pretty strict at detecting song downloads, and they threaten to cut off the network connection of any student caught downloading or sharing prohibited files. There is a gray area regarding downloading music and movies, so be very careful if you decide to partake. The Honor System is not codified; it is based on trust, so do not be surprised if you hear of an Honor Violation coming out of such a situation.

The College Prowler® Grade on
Computers: A-

A high grade in Computers designates that computer labs are available, the computer network is easily accessible, and the campus's computing technology is up-to-date.

Facilities

The Lowdown On...
Facilities

Campus Size
322 acres

Student Centers
The John W. Elrod University Commons

Main Libraries
James G. Leyburn Library
Law Library
Science Library

Service & Maintenance Staff
131

Popular Places to Chill
BDG (Baker-Davis Gilliam) quad
Café
Commerce School computer lab
Commons living room
Front lawn
Graham-Lees "quad" (courtyard)
Porch

Bar on Campus
None

Bowling on Campus
None

Coffeehouse on Campus
The Café

Movie Theater on Campus
The Commons Theater

Favorite Things To Do
Frisbee, football, tanning, bocce ball, and snow angels on the front lawn; late-night runs to the Commons for junk food; frat parties; packing the stands for Parents' Weekend and Homecoming football games; intramural basketball games in the Warner Center; catching free movies in the Commons; a cappella concerts in Lee Chapel and the Commons.

Pump iron or do aerobics in the Fitness Center, catch some acoustic guitar or a comedian on select weeknights in the Commons, and take in big hits in the movie theater. For a more sophisticated evening, grab a date and head to the Lenfest Center for a performance of Shakespeare, jazz, or chorale music.

Did You Know?

Washington and Lee's libraries contain over one million hard-cover volumes and electronic documents, plus over 6,000 serial subscriptions. Get busy reading!

The Fitness Center holds 38 cardiovascular training stations and 13,000 lbs. of free and fixed weights

Students Speak Out On...
Facilities

Q Excellent Facilities
The commons are beautiful, convenient, luxurious, and have everything you need. The library was recently renovated and is a great place to hang out and study. Classroom buildings are good and the older ones are in the process of renovation. The gym is nice, but the fitness center is a bit small and gets overcrowded at times. Overall, the campus is extremely beautiful, and they go to great lengths around here to keep it that way. They do a stellar job - definitely one of the most beautiful campuses you will ever visit.

Q The school is trying really hard to create options for independent, non-Greek students, and the Commons helps out a lot, with the theater, the foosball tables, and the big TV.

Q The Science Center is phenomenal. I really like how they combine all the scientific departments into one building, which facilitates conversations across disciplines and a general prevailing attitude of teamwork and cooperation among different faculty.

Q Many of the classrooms are in historical sites, so they are kept in immaculate condition—though historical furniture is not the most comfortable to sit in for long periods of time.

Q We have a bowling alley nearby, a movie theater that's a two-minute walk from campus, an outdoor venue called the Lime Kiln (think concerts and wine tasting festivals) within walking distance, and even a drive-in movie theater a little ways outside of town.

Q We have only one dining hall and one co-op, so dining options are rather limited. Social options are also very limited, though it is getting a lot better. The social life revolves around the fraternity system, which is unfortunate. But with the new Commons, new movies are shown almost every day of the week, and bands are brought in to play on weekends. There are a lot more options now than there were when I was a freshman.

Q Students are going to want to visit Kroger, Food Lion, or Wal-Mart for almost anything and everything they may need.

Q There is a small movie theater in town, but the Elrod Commons has a theater and shows movies recently taken off the big screen, a month to three months after they show in theaters. The school is also trying to have comedy shows once a week, and brings bands and speakers to campus pretty often as well.

The College Prowler Take On...
Facilities

A few years ago, the facilities at W&L were seriously lacking. The weight room, for example, looked like something off the set of Rocky (before he made it big): torn carpet, smeared windows, and rusty equipment. Now, thanks to a spending binge that would make a Washington politician proud, W&L's campus sports a sparkling new exercise facility, a $30 million Student Commons, and a journalism school wired for the 21st century. Students can play pool and catch Monday Night Football in the Commons or break a sweat in the pristine Fitness Center. Construction on a state-of-the-art, 60,000-square-foot music and arts center, Lenfest Center, was completed in August 2006. The school works hard at making up for what Lexington lacks in the area of social entertainment. The administration has been investing a lot of money into building up the school and creating an environment that appeals to students.

The University has been extremely cognizant of improving the buildings that have been once seen as a blight on campus. The $2.5 million Leyburn Library improvement project has just been finished, and the improvement of Newcomb Hall is in progress for next year. As far as buying things on campus, the school bookstore has some of the basic toiletries, but for the most part, students have to go off campus to find food and other random odds and ends. With all that W&L has been doing lately, students wouldn't be surprised if their problems with these facilities were soon addressed as well.

The College Prowler® Grade on
Facilities: B+

A high Facilities grade indicates that the campus is aesthetically pleasing and well-maintained; facilities are state-of-the-art, and libraries are exceptional. Other determining factors include the quality of both athletic and student centers and an abundance of things to do on campus.

Campus Dining

The Lowdown On...
Campus Dining

Meal Plan Available?
Yes

Average Meal Plan Cost
$5125 per year

Average Meals/Week
19

Freshman Meal Plan Required?
Yes

24-Hour Dining
None

Dining Halls & Campus Restaurants

The Brief Stop at the Law School
Location: School of Law
Food: Salad bar, sandwiches, pastries
Hours: Monday–Thursday 7:45 a.m.–5:30 p.m., Friday 7:45 a.m.–3:30 p.m.

Café 77/Emporium
Location: University Commons
Food: Burgers, salads, subs, junk food
Hours: Monday–Friday 7:30 a.m.–12 a.m., Saturday 9 a.m.–12 a.m., Sunday 1 p.m.–12 a.m.

The Marketplace
Location: University Commons
Food: American, with periodic international-themed dinners
Hours: Monday–Friday 7:15 a.m.–7 p.m., Saturday–Sunday 11 a.m.–7 p.m.

Student Favorites
Café 77
The Marketplace

Off-Campus Places to Use Flex Money
None

Did You Know?

 Students with special dietary needs just need to talk to the chefs, and they will set up meal plans that meet the requirements.

Students Speak Out On...
Campus Dining

Q I think the food is okay; people just complain because they feel the need to complain about something.

Q The quality of the food in the Commons is excellent. At the fraternity houses, the quality drops a little, but is still pretty good. On campus, there is plenty of variety for the health-conscious.

Q Nothing on campus is open 24 hours, and something of this nature could be a big help to students studying all night.

Q The food is pretty good. The D-hall has been upgraded to the Marketplace, and there are more options for students. There is always a variety of pizza. There is also a deli bar, a different type of soup every day, a salad bar, hot dogs, burgers, and grilled chicken. The main course varies from day to day.

Q The Marketplace hosts regular theme dinners—for instance, Mardi Gras dinner, Indian dinner, and African dinner, just to name a few. There is also a wide variety of drinks, including sodas, juice, water, power drinks, coffee, tea, hot chocolate, and milk.

Q I think the food is really good, compared to the ones I have seen in other places (also a lot better than the old D-hall). There's always deli, grill, or pizza if students don't like the hot meal.

Q The food at W&L basically depends on what year you are. The Marketplace, mainly where freshmen eat, offers a wide variety of choices at each meal. Some upperclassmen choose to eat in the Marketplace during the rest of their time at W&L. Our Café, the short-order restaurant that is open most of the day, is great for meals and snacks. Many upperclassmen eat at fraternities or sororities. Each house has a different cook, and there is enough variety in the food choice to make it worthwhile. The meal plans are for those who may just want a few meals a week, as well as for those who can't even boil their own water.

Q The addition of the new dining hall has greatly improved cafeteria food relative to dining services when I was a freshman, but the new Café has actually taken a step backwards from the old co-op.

The College Prowler Take On...
Campus Dining

Students on campus have a few options when it comes time to grab some munchies or a sit-down meal. The student dining hall, or "Marketplace" (its regal, official name) has a popular hot dog and hamburger bar, plus fresh deli sandwiches on demand. The Café, also in the Commons, is more affordable than the Marketplace (an average meal costs between $4 and $7), and the food is generally tasty. The specials add a little variety, which is otherwise lacking. Favorites include the Sunrise breakfast sandwiches, breadsticks, and beef cheesesteak subs. The daily specials are usually yummy. As an added bonus, the Café has all of the caffeine and chocolate a tired student could hope for: Red Bull, candy bars, and coffee on tap.

Freshmen have to purchase the full meal plan, 21 meals per week. Very few students actually eat all this food—for example, many feel that sleep is often more valuable than breakfast; so some of this money goes down the drain. But upperclassmen can choose from a variety of meal plans, some of them much less expensive than the freshman plan. One option that a lot of students do involves eating at their respective fraternity or sorority. The Greek houses each have their own cook and offer a variety of different foods to eat.

The College Prowler® Grade on
Campus Dining: B

The grade on Campus Dining addresses the quality of both school-owned dining halls and independent on-campus restaurants as well as the price, availability, and variety of food.

Off-Campus Dining

The Lowdown On...
Off-Campus Dining

Restaurant Listings

Applebee's
Food: American
870 N. Lee Hwy., at the Holiday Inn Express
(540) 463-2306
www.applebees.com
Price: $8–$15

Aunt Sarah's Pancake House
Food: Breakfast, sandwiches
2813 N. Lee Hwy.
(540) 464-5227
www.auntsarahspancake-house.com
Price: $5–$10

Berky's Restaurant
Food: Breakfast, buffet
2516 N. Lee Hwy.
(540) 463-3478
Price: $5–$10

Bistro on Main
Food: Contemporary
8 N. Main St.
(540) 464-4888
www.bistro-lexington.com
Price: $15–$25

Café Michel
Food: American, French
640 N. Lee Hwy.
(540) 464-4119
www.michelcafe.com
Price: $10–$25

Crystal Chinese Restaurant
Food: Chinese
1225 N. Lee Hwy.
(540) 464-1828
Price: $5–$10

Daily Grind
Food: Coffee, smoothies, sandwiches
23 S. Jefferson St.
(540) 462-6003
Price: $3–$8

Domino's Pizza
Food: Pizza
23 S. Jefferson St.
(540) 463-7375
www.dominos.com
Price: $5–$10
Cool Features: The best spot for late-night eating close to campus. Carry out or delivery only.

Don Tequila
Food: Tex-Mex
455 E. Nelson St.
(540) 463-3289
Price: $5–$10
Cool Features: Occasional mariachi band performances on Wednesday night

Frank's Pizza & Subs
Food: Italian
511 E. Nelson St.
(540) 463-7575
Price: $5–$10

Healthy Foods Co-op and Cafe
Food: Organic, vegetarian, whole foods
110 W. Washington St.
(540) 463-6954
healthyfoodscoop.org
Price: $5–$15

A Joyful Spirit Café
Food: Breakfast, wraps, salads
26 S. Main St.
(540) 463-4191
Price: $5–$10

Lexington Coffee Shop
Food: Coffee, baked goods
9 W. Washington St.
(540) 464-6586
www.damnfinecoffee.net
Price: $3–$5

Macado's Restaurant & Bar
Food: American, sandwiches
30 N. Main St.
(540) 464-8201
www.macados.net
Price: $8–$15

Naples Pizza, Pasta & Subs
Food: Italian
1213 N. Lee Highway
(540) 463-3399
Price: $5–$15

The Palms
Food: American
101 W. Nelson St.
(540) 463-7911
www.thepalmslexington.com
Price: $10–$20

Papa John's Pizza
Food: Pizza
114 E. Midland Trail
(540) 463-7777
www.papajohns.com
Price: $5–$15

Ruby Tuesday
Food: American
1120 N. Lee Hwy.
(540) 463-2094
www.rubytuesday.com
Price: $8–$15

Salerno's
Food: Pizza, Italian
115 S. Jefferson St.
(540) 463-5757
Price: $5–$10
Cool Features: Packed on Wednesdays for $5.95 large cheese pizzas

Sheridan Livery Inn
Food: American, seafood
35 N. Main St.
(540) 464-1887
web.mac.com/fbenincasa/index/home.html
Price: $15–$25
Cool Features: Top place for a fancy date

Smokin' Jim's Firehouse BBQ
Food: Barbecue
107 N. Main St.
(540) 463-2283
Price: $5–$10
Cool Features: The eponymous Jim makes ribs so tender they can be cut with a plastic spoon

Southern Inn Restaurant
Food: Contemporary American
37 S. Main St.
(540) 463-3612
www.southerninn.com
Price: $15–$20

Sweet Things Ice Cream Shoppe
Food: Ice cream
106 W. Washington St.
(540) 463-6055
Price: $2–$5
Cool Features: Amazing pumpkin pie ice cream

Sweet Treats Bakery
Food: Baked goods, breakfast
19 W. Washington St.
(540) 463-3611
www.sweettreatsbakery.net
Price: $5–$10

Waffle House
Food: Breakfast, sandwiches
8 Maury River Rd.

(540) 463-6223
www.wafflehouse.com
Price: $4–$8

Wendy's
Food: Fast food
531 E. Nelson St.
(540) 463-5005
www.wendys.com
Price: $3–$6

Best Asian
Crystal Chinese Restaurant

Best Breakfast
Aunt Sarah's Pancake House
A Joyful Spirit Café
Sweet Treats Bakery

Best Healthy
Healthy Foods Co-op
A Joyful Spirit Café

Best Pizza
Domino's Pizza
Frank's
Naples
Papa John's
Salerno's

Best Wings
Domino's Pizza
Macado's

Best Place to Take Your Parents
Bistro
Café Michel
Sheridan Livery Inn
The Southern Inn

24-Hour Dining
Berky's Restaurant
Waffle House

Other Places to Check Out
The Stop-In

Grocery Stores
Food Lion
84 E. Midland Trail
(540) 464-5026

Kroger
422 E. Nelson St.
(540) 464-3309

Wal-Mart
1233 Rt. 11/N. Lee Hwy.
(540) 464-3535

Did You Know?

Lexington hosts an annual food and wine festival that features local cuisine, live music, and wine from over a dozen Virginia wineries. Bottoms up!

Stick around over February Break and enjoy Chocolate Lovers' Weekend, complete with chocolate-cooking demonstrations and chocolate-themed dinners at some of Lexington's swanky restaurants. Perfect for Valentine's Day.

Students Speak Out On...
Off-Campus Dining

Q You'll Get Bored Fast
There are several options in Lex but they do get old after awhile. The variety is actually decent for a town of this size. Cost differs by place, but most are reasonable. Be sure to check out Frank's and (for a night out) Cafe Michel's

Q
The cost of living in Lexington is quite low, and you can get some pretty solid meals for not a lot of money.

Q
Not many food cultures are represented here, but variety really depends on what you are comparing it to. If you compare it to New York City, where I'm from, then no, there is not a lot of variety. But Lexington has really expanded its food choices in the last few years.

Q
Sheridan Livery, perhaps the most expensive restaurant in town, has really good food. This is particularly suitable for a dinner date before a formal or semi-formal. Don Tequila's, a Mexican restaurant, is great if you're into spicy stuff, and allows for a more casual, relaxed outing. Likewise, the Palms, restaurant by day, bar by night, is great for casual dates.

Q
My favorite restaurant is definitely Frank's Pizza and Subs. I go every Sunday with a group of friends, and the pasta dishes never get old. For Chinese, Crystal Palace is the place to go—can't get enough of their buffet. For a date, I'd go to the Sheridan Livery or the Southern Inn—both are classy, but not pretentious. In terms of 24-hours, the only place is the Stop-In and Wal-Mart. However, since our parties start early, they often end in time to hit up Smokin' Jim's BBQ or Wendy's late-night.

Q Berky's at Lee High Truck Stop and Waffle House are open 24 hours. I have spent nights studying at Berky's a few times.

Q In terms of cost, there is something for everybody. I find that food here is much cheaper than in a large city, but there are some pricey places around town. There aren't many discounts, but the restaurant managers trust W&L students so much that often, if you're short on cash, they will let you leave with the anticipation that you'll pay them back soon.

Q Café Michel is amazing. The French cuisine is delicious, and the food is about 23 dollars a plate. The red snapper with crab and champagne sauce is the best seafood I've had this far inland. For cheaper food, the Palms is the best restaurant. The hamburgers are wonderful.

The College Prowler Take On...
Off-Campus Dining

The restaurant offerings in Lexington run the whole spectrum of culinary delight (and dislike), although some students are not satisfied with the offerings. On the sophisticated side, Lexington has the Sheridan Livery Inn ($25 a plate—ouch). Despite, or because of, its price tag, it's always an impressive destination reserved either for really special dates or a place to take the parents when they are paying. For more casual outings, Smokin' Jim's Firehouse Barbeque and Salerno's are student favorites. Most students can find what they are craving, or if they really have motivation, will take the hour to drive to Roanoke to find it.

New eating (and drinking) places are sprouting up in Lexington: a corner bakery, an alternative coffee shop, a French restaurant, and a sushi bar are the latest additions. But beware: just about everything closes down at 9 or 10 p.m. So W&L students often end up relying on Domino's or the Stop-In to feed their late-night cravings. There are a couple of other late-night options open for students, the Waffle House and Berky's Restaurant, which offer 24-hour dining; however, some students find going to these places to be a little sketchy, so they stick to the late-night Wendy's window.

The College Prowler® Grade on
Off-Campus Dining: B+

A high Off-Campus Dining grade implies that off-campus restaurants are affordable, accessible, and worth visiting. Other factors include the variety of cuisine and the availability of alternative options (vegetarian, vegan, kosher).

Campus Housing

The Lowdown On...
Campus Housing

On-Campus Housing Available?
Yes

Campus Housing Capacity
1,181

Average Housing Costs
$3,630

Number of Dormitories
4

Number of Campus-Owned Apartments
1

Dormitories

Davis Hall
Floors: 3
Number of Occupants: 72
Bathrooms: Shared
Coed: Yes
Residents: Freshmen
Room Types: Doubles
Special Features: Bike rack, Ethernet, in-room sink, loftable beds, wireless Internet

Gaines Hall
Floors: 4
Number of Occupants: 180
Bathrooms: Private by suite
Coed: Yes
Residents: Freshmen and upperclassmen
Room Types: Suites (singles, doubles)
Special Features: Air conditioning, cable TV, carpeting, common rooms, Ethernet, laundry facilities, walk-in closet, wireless Internet

Gilliam Hall
Floors: 4
Number of Occupants: 88
Bathrooms: Shared
Coed: Yes
Residents: Freshmen
Room Types: Singles, doubles
Special Features: Bike rack, cable TV, Ethernet, in-room sink, laundry facilities, loftable beds, wireless Internet. Home to Student Health Center.

Graham-Lees Hall
Floors: 4
Number of Occupants: 254
Bathrooms: Shared
Coed: Yes
Residents: Freshmen
Room Types: Singles, doubles
Special Features: Cable TV, Ethernet, laundry facilities, loftable beds, wireless Internet

Theme Housing
Floors: Varies
Number of Occupants: Varies
Bathrooms: Shared by residents (International House has gender-specific bathrooms)
Coed: Yes
Residents: Upperclassmen
Room Types: Singles, doubles
Special Features: Theme housing gives upperclassmen the opportunity to live with other students with similar interests. Options include the John Chavis House (African American community), International House, Outing Club House, and Casa Hispanica (Spanish House).

Campus-Owned Apartments
Woods Creek Apartments
Number of Units: 40
Bathrooms: Private by unit
Coed: Yes, but individual suites are single-sex
Residents: Upperclassmen
Room Types: Three- to five-bedroom apartments (singles)
Special Features: Balconies, kitchenettes, living rooms,

Freshmen Required to Live on Campus?
Yes

Undergrads Living On Campus
43%

Best Dorms
Gilliam (for a more mellow experience)
Graham-Lees (for craziness in a well-lit environment)

Worst Dorms
Davis

What You Get
Bed
Closet
Desk and chair
Dresser
Mirror

Available for Rent
Bed linens
MicroFridges

Also Available
Substance-free halls where residents can agree to set stricter rules about alcohol and smoking are available. Contact the Student Affairs Office at (540) 458-8754.

Did You Know?

About 60 percent of the freshman rooms in Gilliam, Davis, and Graham-Lees residence halls are doubles; the rest are single rooms. W&L students are so sociable!

Students Speak Out On...
Campus Housing

Q No one lives in Gaines or Woods Creek unless they have to (the perks of being an RA). Living on campus sucks. You can't drink, you can't be loud if you want to, and, in general, the living arrangements are just kind of depressing.

Q Crazy stuff goes down in Graham-Lees because everyone lives there, and the halls are so much bigger. We have pizza parties in the hallways, and you can just hang out in the halls until four in the morning.

Q You get the unforgettable dorm experience your freshman year and can roll out of bed at 8:47 and be in class at 9 with a minute to spare.

Q Walking at a normal clip from the dorms, it doesn't take more than five minutes to make it to the main portion of campus, maybe a bit more for the far side where the Science Center is located. You could probably cut this down to three minutes if you made a dash for it.

Q My dorm counselor freshman year was great. I really can't emphasize that enough. He did a splendid job of helping the horde of clueless freshmen on his hall (including me) make it through the pitfalls of their first year. The DC program does a good job of screening out most of the bad apples. I've heard far more good things than bad things.

Q Dorms are incredibly close to classes—closer than any other housing. They are closer than the parking garage that students living off campus use.

Q Freshman housing is a little scary and rather plain, but once you get beyond the first year, housing improves significantly. Upperclass housing is in suite units, so it is like living in an apartment with 2 to 4 other people.

Q My freshman room was a nightmare. It was far too small for a roommate and me to live in. We tried to work it out until Thanksgiving, but then we gave up. The room was just too small—we couldn't even fit our two beds in the room without them blocking the door. On the other hand, when we contacted our Dean of Freshmen about the problem, she resolved all of the issues very quickly. We were each given our own rooms and life became a lot more pleasant. Freshmen are not alone—the administration is there to help them.

The College Prowler Take On...
Campus Housing

W&L students have to live on campus for their first two years at the University (the fraternity and sorority houses, as well as the dorms, qualify as on campus, and are open to sophomores). Students confront a whole range experiences in on-campus housing—sometimes it's good, sometimes it's pretty bad. The rooms themselves are generally unexceptional, so whether students enjoy their accommodations depends a lot on roommates, dorm counselors, and neighbors down the hall. Students can make lasting friendships during their time in the freshman halls. When there are problems, students say that the administration usually gets right on it and resolves issues ranging from roommate problems to space issues.

Of course, some places just seem to be better at creating the full freshman experience—the invigorating sense of meeting a bunch of new people and crashing into adult life, full-speed. Gaines, with its quiet halls and rooms divided into suites, is lacking here, despite its cleanliness and high-class feel. For incoming students, it's best to try a real freshman dorm such as Graham-Lees, which, while not the most attractive building, tends to create the most memorable experiences. After freshman year, students tend to expand to other dorms, such as Woods Creek, which offers more of an off-campus feel; they also have the option of moving into fraternity and sorority houses. Upperclassmen usually don't stay on campus, and they have last pick for housing if they do.

The College Prowler® Grade on
Campus Housing: B

A high Campus Housing grade indicates that dorms are clean, well-maintained, and spacious. Other determining factors include variety of dorms, proximity to classes, and social atmosphere.

Off-Campus Housing

The Lowdown On...
Off-Campus Housing

Undergrads Living Off Campus
57%

Average Rents
Studio: $300
1 BR: $250
2 BR: $500
4 BR: $800

Best Time to Look for a Place
Winter term of freshman year—seriously. Students can wait longer to look, but they may have to rely on friends who already have housing. Best bet is to call real estate offices or ask around—W&L does not provide official help in getting off-campus housing.

Popular Areas
Downtown
Pole Houses
Randolph Street
Tucker Street
Windfall Hill

Students Speak Out On...
Off-Campus Housing

Q **Lucky or Not**
Off campus housing can be spotty. Students often complain of less than desirable landlords. The good part of this, of course, is that you don't have to worry about ruining a rental (aka parties can definitely happen).

Q Since housing is done by a lottery system, and rising sophomores get first pick and seniors get last pick, it is fairly difficult as a senior to get on-campus housing. There isn't really a lack of space, but sometimes seniors end up 'filling in' empty rooms in apartments or suites with random sophomores or juniors who have these empty rooms. This is often less than desirable since people generally like to live with their friends. It all depends on when your number gets picked.

Q Living in a sorority house is certainly fun. You cannot get a lot of work done, but with a library open 24 hours, it is no big deal. In my opinion, though, it should only be done once (if at all). Your grades might suffer, and you might become a huge brat if you are catered in one of the

Q Rent is comparatively inexpensive, but what's nice is that housing options exist for every price range—if one home is too expensive, you can easily find another, cheaper place to rent.

Q Off-campus housing probably is cheaper than living in the dorms. I pay $300 a month for a house in the country, with 5 bedrooms, 2 bathrooms and a basement. I think there are only a handful of places in this country where you could get a deal like that.

Q Students can always find a decent off-campus house to live in. That said, I believe that being a Greek gives you a much better chance to get prime housing.

Q After sophomore year, most W&L students move off campus. It is a good experience for students to learn how to really live on their own. There is plenty of off-campus housing in Lexington and the surrounding area. Students can generally choose how far away from campus they want to live.

Q Off-campus housing ranges in condition from fairly run-down houses to new apartments and houses. The cost of living in Lexington is the cheapest of any college town I have heard of. The rent for my three-bedroom apartment is $650 per month. The area seems to have a relatively low crime rate, as there is very little incident of theft and virtually no safety issues.

The College Prowler Take On...
Off-Campus Housing

For a small town, Lexington and the surrounding area provide a good deal of off-campus housing for students who want to venture out. Lists of housing are passed through fraternities and sororities, but even non-Greek students who are willing to invest some effort can usually find what they need. The quality of the housing varies wildly, however, from new houses on hilltops outside of town to apartments in poorly-lit and run-down mansions. Plus, students who want to control where they end up have to start looking for off-campus digs extremely early because of the rush of students to get off-campus in their junior years. This can be a serious hassle, since the school does not provide official assistance for students looking for off-campus housing.

The cost of living in Lexington or Rockbridge County is low, so students who find roommates to share the cost shouldn't have to worry about exorbitant rents. The off-campus housing is generally safe, courtesy of Lexington's low crime rate, but theft can occur in town when students get careless. Students should know that many of the country roads further away from campus dip and curve around rolling hills and sharp bends. Driving is treacherous when it snows, which can be a problem when W&L doesn't cancel class. It's a consideration a lot of students try to take when searching for a good place off campus.

The College Prowler® Grade on

Off-Campus Housing: A-

A high grade in Off-Campus Housing indicates that apartments are of high quality, close to campus, affordable, and easy to secure.

Diversity

The Lowdown On...
Diversity

African American
3%

Asian American
3%

Hispanic
3%

International
5%

Native American
0%

White
85%

Unknown
0%

Out-of-State Students
85%

Faculty Diversity
African American: 4%
Asian American: 3%
Hispanic: 1%
International: 0%
Native American: 0%
White: 90%
Unknown: 1%

Historically Black College/University?
No

Student Age Breakdown
Under 18: 5%
18-19: 41%
20-21: 36%
22-24: 11%
25+: 8%

Economic Status

From all appearances, this is a well-off campus. However, do not be discouraged if you do not feel you fall into one of the traditional income brackets. The University has been using the Johnson Scholarship to allow academically deserving students to pursue their education at Washington and Lee regardless of their income.

Gay Pride

There is not a large gay presence on campus, but many students here seem fairly accepting of others who have come out. A chapter of the Gay-Straight Alliance was established in the fall of 2002, and since then has brought a lot of attention to the issue.

Most Common Religions

Catholic, Episcopal, Presbyterian, and Methodist, in declining order. The General's Christian Fellowship and Reformed University Fellowship are the two largest Christian groups, and they often attract about 100 people for services. Students declaring a religious preference hit 70 percent in 1998, but that percentage has now declined to 55 percent. Just over half of all undergrads list a Christian religious preference.

Political Activity

W&L students are no longer as reliably conservative as they once were—there is now some competition on the political front. During the 2004 election year, Young Democrats helped to get out the vote for the local party, and College Republicans countered with their own speakers and volunteer drives. But the political scene is typically fairly low-key: students from both sides can cooperate and mingle with each other. You hardly ever see a protest or demonstration of any kind.

Minority Clubs on Campus

Minority students are very active in several organizations that know how to have good, clean fun. The Minority Students

Association helps to promote minority recruitment and sponsors an annual cabaret, complete with great food in a swanky setting—bring a date and dance to soul and R&B music till the wee hours. Club Asia, after getting off the ground just recently, put on a very cool cultural fair (hint: lots of martial arts weapons). The Student Association for International Learning (SAIL) helps international students get accustomed to Lexington. It also sponsors a Model United Nations and international relief projects, as well as internationally-themed parties.

Students Speak Out On...
Diversity

Q Diversity: "White and Loaded" Not Always the Norm
While W&L is still deeply enamored of its bow-ties, khakis, pearls, and Vineyard Vines, there is definitely diversity on campus. This diversity has been an upward trend of late. As a First-Year myself I know students of all different backgrounds and ethnicities. A very stern talk given to all First-Years at the beginning of the year, warning against racist behavior, might make one think that this behavior is common but as far as I can tell that is simply not true. (Then again, I am white and loaded so my opinion can only go so far). Yes -- there are still the white and loaded at W&L (who else would pay for all the parties?) But people of all backgrounds are welcome.

Q The multicultural groups seem to form cliques and hang out with each other. You don't see a lot of mingling across different cultures.

Q Students naturally tend to segregate themselves, mainly because of the Greek system. 'I'm an SAE' or 'I'm a Chi-O' is almost always attached to somebody's identity, whether it's good or bad. Don't get me wrong, the Greek system is great, and I really enjoy it. But it certainly has its stereotypes.

Q For the most part, people are tolerant. I haven't confronted any intolerance myself.

Q Unfortunately, this is not a very diverse campus on a broad scope, but it's certainly improving. The main demographic stereotype here is southern, rich, and white.

However, just this Parents' Weekend, my mom commented on how noticeable the increase in African-American and Asian students was. This is great, because W&L has a

Q Lack of diversity is a major deficiency at W&L, but it is changing for the better. Minority groups are not abundant enough. I wish we had way more diversity in socioeconomic backgrounds, intellectual and cultural viewpoints, and national origins. Right now, W&L is too homogeneous, and you have to actively seek intellectual stimulation. However, the University is taking steps to increase diversity, and I think the trend is toward more intelligent students as well as more interesting and unique ones.

Q There is tolerance of different races and ethnicities, but don't expect much more than just tolerance. Most people don't go out of their way to embrace. Don't get me wrong, there is very little open discrimination on campus, but you don't often see minority students at Greek parties unless they are members of a Greek organization.

Q Without a doubt, most of the student body is rich and dresses a certain way. This does not mean a student of a different economic status cannot be comfortable here. If you are comfortable standing out in a crowd, then you will be fine.

The College Prowler Take On...
Diversity

Washington and Lee has acquired a partially-deserved reputation for being a place where everyone talks the same (in a southern drawl), dresses the same (sandals, pastel polo shirts with popped collars), votes the same (Republican), and looks the same (white). However, much of that may be changing. The percentage of minority students has been on the rise and is around 10 percent. A dean of multicultural affairs was hired last year to spread the word that W&L welcomes minorities. There have been serious discussions about forming an African American Studies program, which would involve faculty and students from a range of departments, including history, politics, music, and English. There are also rumblings about students forming chapters of historically African American sororities in the near future, but this seems to be farther off.

In keeping with the "nostalgic for Reagan" motif, W&L harbors an active and well-connected chapter of College Republicans, officially the largest student group on campus (they "put the 'dubya' in 'dubyanell'"). But the Young Democrats showed a lot of life in the 2004 election season, working local fundraisers and bringing speakers to campus. W&L fosters a vibrant and growing community of clubs and organizations, from the Boxing Club to the Knitting Club to the Williams Investment Society, in which students wheel and deal with $1 million of the University's endowment. While students find diversity in interests, the numbers really don't lie; W&L just isn't too diverse, but it is working on it. The $100 million Johnson Scholarship has allowed many different backgrounds of student to attend, and everyone at the University seems to be embracing it.

The College Prowler® Grade on
Diversity: D

A high grade in Diversity indicates that ethnic minorities and international students have a notable presence on campus and that students of different economic backgrounds, religious beliefs, and sexual preferences are well-represented.

Guys & Girls

The Lowdown On...
Guys & Girls

Female Undergrads
50%

Male Undergrads
50%

Birth Control Available?
Yes: At the Student Health Center.

Social Scene
The social scene is huge here—students shouldn't expect to lock themselves in their room and study all the time. Even studying and writing papers sometimes become social activities, as students congregate in the C-School or J-School to commiserate. Introverted kids have a tougher time finding a niche in the midst of pretty frantic social activity, especially during the first term or two, but most eventually seem to adjust. Similarly, non-Greeks and students who never go out to frat parties can feel like the life of the University is passing them by. Advice: students should at least try the Greek scene a little bit, and sample the growing options for alternative entertainment if the frat scene doesn't measure up. The Commons has become the central meeting place on campus—students filter through by the hundreds every hour.

Hookups or Relationships?
The dating scene is extremely sparse until junior and senior years when some students move into steady relationships. Hookups are predominant on campus throughout the four years.

Dress Code
Preppy dress is standard issue here. When the weather permits, ladies often wear skirts and spring dresses to class, accessorized with calf boots or heels. On balmy days, the stereotypical W&L man sports a slightly ruffled haircut, a polo shirt (preferably pastel), khakis, and sandals. (In nastier weather, the campus runs amok in grey North Face jackets). However, mad props to the iconoclasts who wear cowboy boots and suede jackets to class. You know who you are.

Students Speak Out On...
Guys & Girls

Q Hook-Up
Do not go to W&L looking for a soul mate, long walks on the beach, or someone to enjoy long romantic bubble baths with (ok, no one looks for that, but you get the point). But seriously, it is really not a dating community. I have heard rumors of upperclassmen couples (people who actually refer to themselves as boyfriend and girlfriend *gasp* but I cannot confirm this). However if you enjoy hooking up, this is the place for you. Guys are awarded the highest honor, that of "6-Star General" when they have slept with a girl from each sorority. All this can be bad or good, depending on the way you look at it. Either way, its a ton of fun *wink*;)   Oh, looks!! We are preppy, very preppy. We do not wear sweat pants. We wear pearls often. We are rather good-looking, but of course this can differ. We are the best.

Q
There aren't any set visiting hours for members of the opposite sex in the dorms. Individual freshmen halls or suites can set policies if they want to do so, but everyone tends just to operate under the general rules of common courtesy.

Q
The division after freshman year between frats and sororities leads to mutated relationships, and it is very difficult to date someone in the conventional sense. People are very focused on status and popularity, rather than platonic intimacy or actually getting to know each other. Maybe this is a vestige of times when W&L was not coed and women were brought in from other schools.

Q Student Health Services both provides and encourages contraception very actively. You can get free condoms at the Student Health Center or through 25 cent vending machines if you'd like anonymity. Also, the peer health education group, LIFE, puts out condom baskets in the dorms, frat, and sorority houses prior to every major party weekend.

Q Very few people roll up to class in sweats. Unlike at most campuses, our students show up to class completely decked out—women with the latest fashions complete with heels and jewelry and men with khakis and polo shirts. Everyone has a bad morning, and so you do see people with sweats and pajamas on during the day, but mainly on Thursdays after a rough Wednesday night.

Q There are way more attractive girls than attractive guys. I've seen gorgeous girls compete for guys they wouldn't look twice at if we were at a state school.

Q While there might be consequences for being caught fooling around in, say, Lee Chapel, outside of that, the worst penalty you would pay for being caught in an intimate moment in your dorm room would be some mockery from your hallmates (or congratulations, as the case may be).

Q The male-to-female ratio doesn't really play into the social scene, since the ratio is about even. But it is like you're back in high school, because W&L is so small, almost everyone has hooked up or dated one another (lots of overlapping, which can be obnoxious and lead to high school-type dramatics).

The College Prowler Take On...
Guys & Girls

W&L is blessed with more than its fair share of attractive ladies. Perhaps it's a "Southun thang," but most of these ladies take great pride in fixing themselves up for every special (and not-so-special) occasion. The guys can be impressive when they want to be: a blazer, khakis, and a tie—preferably a bow tie—are standard. But because too many guys falter in the personal grooming department, the girls rate a little higher—sorry boys. Students give mixed signals about whether W&L is a promiscuous campus. But a huge online survey sponsored by the school in March 2004—the National College Health Assessment—showed that, on average, students here are actually less sexually active than their peers nationwide.

Men and women at W&L seem to treat each other with respect: a tradition of gentility and courtesy persists. Ladies should expect regular, if not universal, door-holding from guys here. Now the bad news: the National College Health Assessment mentioned above also indicated that unwanted sexual touching and attempted rape goes unreported at W&L. The number of female students who reported experiencing unwanted feel-ups or attempted rape was about twice the average at the other 73 schools surveyed. School administrators are working with students, some of whom have founded abuse-awareness groups, like One in Four and the Moustache Society, to see just how deep the problem of sexual misconduct runs and how to fix it.

Guys: B

The College Prowler® Grade on Guys & Girls

A high grade for Guys or Girls indicates that the students on campus is attractive, smart, friendly, and engaging, and that the school has a decent gender ratio.

Girls: B+

Athletics

The Lowdown On...
Athletics

Athletic Association
NAA
NCAA

Athletic Division
NCAA Division III (with football)

Athletic Conferences
Football: Old Dominion Athletic Conference
Basketball: Old Dominion Athletic Conference

School Colors
Royal blue and white

School Nickname/ Mascot
The Generals

Men Playing Varsity Sports
344: 39%

Women Playing Varsity Sports
226: 26%

Men's Varsity Sports
Baseball
Basketball
Cross country
Football
Golf
Lacrosse
Soccer
Swimming
Tennis
Track and field
Wrestling

Women's Varsity Sports
Basketball
Cross country
Equestrian
Field hockey
Lacrosse
Soccer
Swimming
Tennis
Track and field
Volleyball

Intramurals
Basketball
Bowling
Dodgeball
Flag football
Floor hockey
Golf
Kickball
Mini-golf
Racquetball
Soccer
Softball
Table tennis
Tennis
Volleyball
Weightlifting

Club Sports
Badminton
Ballroom dance
Baseball
Basketball (men's and women's)
Brazilian Jiu Jitsu
Croquet
Cycling
Equestrian
Fencing
Field hockey
Golf
Gymnastics
Ice hockey
Judo
Kendo
Lacrosse (men's and women's)
Martial arts
Outdoor
Racquetball
Rock Climbing
Rowing
Rugby (men's and women's)
Running
Sail and paddle
Sailing
Shotokan Karate
Soccer (men's and women's)
Softball
Surfing

Swimming
Synchronized swimming
Tae Kwon Do
Tennis
Triathlon
Ultimate Frisbee (men's and women's)
Volleyball
Water polo
Weightlifting
Wrestling
Yoga

Athletic Fields & Facilities

Alston Parker Watt Field
Cap'n Dick Smith Field
Cy Twombly Pool
Dick Miller Cross Country Course
Doremus Gymnasium
Duchossois Tennis Center
Lexington Country Club
Mathis Wrestling Room
Outdoor Tennis Courts
W&L Turf Field
Warner Center Complex
Wilson Field

Most Popular Sports
Men's lacrosse, club rugby

Most Overlooked Teams
Football—they won the ODAC Championship in 2007 and had two rebuilding years but should be back on top either this year or next.

School Spirit
Even if it's not expressed in the usual ways (thousands of screaming, belly-painted fans at basketball games), W&L students have a lot of school spirit. No matter what they study, students come together for all kinds of activities, from the political craziness of Mock Convention every four years to the prom-night extravaganza of Fancy Dress to the sweaty yard work of spring service days. Students also care about what the University will be like for the students who come after them, which explains the sometimes-obsessive debates about alcohol policies, the academic calendar, crackdowns on fraternities, and the honor system. The one real weakness in the school spirit department is the lack of connection between Greek and non-Greek students. Relations between the two groups are usually not hostile—they're usually friendly, actually—but sometimes these students disagree strongly about how the University should design itself for the future. This saps some of the unity and goodwill that has been built up at W&L over the years.

Getting Tickets
No tickets required!

Best Place to Take a Walk
Woods Creek trails—curves around the wooded back campus and follows the slow-moving creek. Especially nice in the spring and early fall.

Did You Know?

 About 1 in 6 Washington and Lee students are varsity athletes, and about 3 in 4 participate in intramural sports.

Students Speak Out On...
Athletics

Q There's Something for Everybody
Like any town in America, you have your good and your bad. For the most part, off-campus housing is easy to find and relatively nice (unless you live in one of the Greek associated houses). Safety is definitely not a problem overall. Most people leave their house/apartment unlocked.

Q School spirit with regards to sports is unfortunately low. At a school based around tradition, it's sad that more people don't go to games and support their classmates.

Q The student athletes have a good balance between taking the sport they play seriously, and also realizing that it is important to do well in school. Coaches are very understanding of the heavy workload that student athletes have. This doesn't seem to take away from the competitiveness of most of the teams, as they still perform well.

Q The lacrosse games are probably the best-attended events on campus (which really doesn't say much). Soccer gets a good number of fans on the weekends, relatively speaking, but rarely during weekdays. In comparison to the other ODAC teams that we play against in soccer, though, we do have probably one of the best fan bases.

Q Athletes work hard and deserve a good fan base, and it is hard to make it out to all of the games, but the general attitude of most athletes is that not enough fans show up. This is either a result of the lack of emphasis our school places on athletics, or just the sheer volume of work that most students have, which doesn't allow them to attend games, especially on the weekdays.

Q Intramural football and softball is very popular among the frats and law students. Rugby is a very popular club team, and has a sort of groupie following.

Q The overall attitude is probably different from that of larger schools. At W&L, you know most of the people playing on the field personally. Most of the serious fans of W&L sports are the friends of the athletes. As a whole, I'd have to say that W&L students are apathetic towards our sports teams.

Q The attitude toward sports could be much stronger than it is. The heavy workload that students have is probably the main reason for this. The students who don't play sports occasionally show up to some of the home games, depending on the sport, but typically the fan base comprises mostly other athletes who have a day off or are playing later that day.

The College Prowler Take On...
Athletics

Washington and Lee puts the "student" in "student athlete." The University doesn't award athletic scholarships, and athletes are expected to carry their academic weight. This sometimes makes it tough for W&L to field successful teams, particularly in football and basketball. But in some sports—including lacrosse, women's soccer, and tennis—W&L's dominance is unquestioned (or so the athletes will tell you). Attendance is pretty light at most sporting events, but people turn out en masse for Homecoming and Parents' Weekend football games. No tickets are required for athletic events—just find a seat and start cheering. Unfortunately, W&L tradition mandates that spectators leave football games after the first half. Alas, school spirit only runs so deep.

W&L also realizes the importance of athletics to students. Besides just having the Division III varsity sports, the college also offers intramurals and requires students to take gym classes to keep in shape. W&L sponsors a variety of intramural (IM) sports, from basketball to flag football to softball. Combined with club sports, this gives nearly every student an opportunity to play a sport on some level. A lot of clubs, fraternities, and sororities form intramural teams to socialize and have some fun. W&L tries to provide its students with a workout for both mind and body.

The College Prowler® Grade on
Athletics: C+

A high grade in Athletics indicates that students have school spirit, that sports programs are respected, that games are well-attended, and that intramurals are a prominent part of student life.

Nightlife

The Lowdown On...
Nightlife

Cheapest Place to Get a Drink
Macado's
The Palms

Primary Areas with Nightlife
Downtown Lexington

Closing Time
2 a.m.

Bar Listings

Diggers (Inside the Southern Inn)
37 S Main St.
(540) 463-3612
Diggers, set inside an up-scale restaurant, is distinctly more buttoned-down: rowdiness is a no-no, unlike at the Palms.

Macado's Restaurant & Bar
30 N. Main St.
Lexington
(540) 464-8201

The Palms
101 W Nelson St.
(540) 463-7911
This is the center of all W&L bar activity. This corner bar is a key mixing place for juniors and seniors, and it can get pretty packed. Slow service is a nagging complaint because of understaffing, but the food is pretty good—especially the burgers.

Other Places to Check Out
Don Tequila
Hunan Garden Restaurant

Local Specialties
The Schooner at Macado's
The Volcano at Hunan's

Favorite Drinking Games
Beer pong/Beirut
Flip cup
Kings

What to Do if You're Not 21
Try fraternity parties or off-campus house parties. Do not try that fake ID—if you're caught, you might get kicked out of school.

Organization Parties
The Minority Students Association throws an annual "cabaret" that is a hoppin' good time, and the International House sponsors DJ parties that are both sketchy and really, really cool. The school also sponsors the Fancy Dress Ball once a year (fancydress.wlu.edu).

Students Speak Out On...
Nightlife

Q The bar scene is almost nonexistent. And if you're not 21, don't bother even trying to go to the bars, because you might get kicked out of school for it. A fake ID is considered an honor violation.

Q If you don't want to drink or be around alcohol, and if this is going to be huge problem for you, go to another school. Seriously, and this isn't meant to turn anyone off of W&L, but drinking is a big part of life here, so you can accept that or reject it. But, you can accept the drinking atmosphere and not drink while you're at the parties. Some of my favorite friends and people on campus don't drink at all, but they're still a blast when you see them out at night.

Q Frat parties are just about it when it comes to nightlife.

Q There are no dance clubs or night clubs and the bar scene is definitely lacking. But since students would get kicked out from W&L if they were caught with fake IDs, there isn't much need for bars.

Q Definitely check out Fancy Dress, our $80,000 answer to prom.

Q Lexington is a small town with extremely limited sources of entertainment outside frat parties. Highlights include a run-down movie theater, a bar that offers poor service and fills up in the blink of an eye, and a downtown area that closes before dusk. Conclusion: it's the frats or nothing at all.

Q As a tour guide, you can't tell a parent that if your son or daughter doesn't drink, this probably isn't the place for them. So you have to tell them about the other options. I know a lot of people who don't drink, and they still have a good time.

Q Frats rule everything here at W&L, and that makes for an amazing party scene with free everything. The bar scene is almost non-existent (only two in town), but who needs bars when there are four or five frat parties going on at any given time?

The College Prowler Take On...
Nightlife

Most of the nightlife at W&L is supplied by fraternity parties. Unlike in some other college towns, the bar scene is pretty sparse, with a grand total of three establishments. The Palms is relatively popular for students over 21—a 21st birthday there is a W&L tradition—but most of the partying still happens in frat basements. The newest restaurant/bar in town, Macado's, is on the rise with student popularity. It is a place where Townies, Veemies, and students from W&L hang out, so it is very diverse. There are some pretty good drink specials, and the food is not half bad either—definitely worth a visit.

To its credit, the University is trying to provide alternative entertainment, with weekly movies in the Student Commons, comedians, and Common Grounds—nights of free music, coffee, and cookies. Off campus, the bowling alley remains a favorite, with unlimited games on Thursday nights. The offerings for students who are not interested in the party scene have also gotten noticeably better in the past four years.

The College Prowler® Grade on
Nightlife: C-

A high grade in Nightlife indicates that there are many bars and clubs in the area that are easily accessible and affordable. Other determining factors include the number of options for the under-21 crowd and the prevalence of house parties.

Greek Life

The Lowdown On...
Greek Life

Undergrad Men in Fraternities
79%

Undergrad Women in Sororities
76%

Number of Fraternities
16

Number of Sororities
8

Fraternities
Alpha Phi Alpha
Beta Theta Pi
Chi Psi
Kappa Alpha
Lambda Chi Alpha
Phi Beta Sigma
Phi Delta Theta
Phi Gamma Delta
Phi Kappa Psi
Phi Kappa Sigma
Pi Kappa Alpha
Pi Kappa Phi
Sigma Alpha Epsilon
Sigma Chi
Sigma Nu
Sigma Phi Epsilon

Sororities
Alpha Delta Pi
Alpha Kappa Alpha
Chi Omega
Delta Sigma Theta
Kappa Alpha Theta
Kappa Delta
Kappa Kappa Gamma
Pi Beta Phi

Multicultural Colonies
Alpha Kappa Alpha (NPHC)
Alpha Phi Alpha (NPHC)
Delta Sigma Theta (NPHC)
Phi Beta Sigma (NPHC)

Other Greek Organizations
Greek Vision Council
Interfraternity Council
Multicultural Greek Council
Order of Omega
Panhellenic Council

Did You Know?

Dave Matthews Band used to play at W&L all the time until they decided to premier their "Crash" album in the Chi Psi basement in the mid-90s. They were booed offstage and have not returned to W&L since then.

Students Speak Out On...
Greek Life

Q Chances are you will fit into at least one of the fraternities or sororities on campus. But, you do not need to join a fraternity or sorority to fit in—just ask some of our more social independents.

Q In my opinion, fraternities are way too important here. Often, guys' friends are determined mainly along frat lines, or at least those in fraternities spend the most time with and live with guys in their frat. Sororities and fraternities, through the rush process, create unnecessary and hurtful barriers. This process can get very competitive and can cause rifts among upperclassmen and freshmen alike. Hopefully the Greek system's importance is starting to decline here.

Q We get our social scene from the frats and sororities because there are no clubs or bars or other colleges of any significance; without the fraternities, this school would be very boring.

Q While going Greek is not imperative, it is a huge step forward in fitting in at W&L. It is hard to fit in without partaking in social functions, mixers, and special weekends, all reserved for inhabitants of the Greek community. Furthermore, each fraternity or sorority member usually finds his or her best friends within that social organization—in the case of the guys, mostly due to the hazards of pledgeship. That being said, independents at W&L are a slow but gathering force. New organizations are sprouting that offer Greek-less activities and healthier recreational activities. Then again, these are usually the kids who can't find anything else to do because they're isolated from the social mainstream.

Q Non-Greeks seem to mind their own business here at W&L. Since they are not directly ostracized, there is no reason for a negative attitude.

Q Non-members can certainly get into fraternity parties (the sororities don't have parties, ever—just date functions). Frat parties are totally open to the public, no charge at all, and there's never anyone at the door deciding who's coming in and who isn't. The beer's free, but then again, it's usually second-rate at best.

Q Parties usually take place in fraternity house basements, and include a cover band, a lesser known band, or a DJ. You'll probably feel more welcome if you know a few members of the house, but you'll never get kicked out. Unless you start some trouble, or you happen to belong to the neighboring Virginia Military Institute, in which case the fratlords will be keeping an extra-close eye on you.

Q A small portion of non-Greeks take advantage of the situation and visit as many houses as possible on party nights. More commonly, however, non-Greeks stick to themselves.

The College Prowler Take On...
Greek Life

Fraternities are absolutely huge at W&L, and have been for generations. About three out of every four guys joins a fraternity. Sororities, since coming to campus in the last decade, now attract about the same percentage of W&L women. What explains this? Students say that the small-town environment, where everything seems to shut down early, pushes them into "frats" or "srats" in order to get their share of nightlife and socializing. Plus, students try to continue the friendships they make in their first term at W&L; groups of friends often decide to join the same fraternity together. Despite the best efforts of the school administration to provide alternative entertainment, the Greek system still drives the social scene. The frats hold parties nearly every weekend, and lay it all out for a few special occasions (Homecoming, Christmas Weekend, Parents' Weekend). Some of the more famous shindigs include Lamba Chi's Tropical Party (complete with a two-story waterfall), Phi Kappa Phi's Forties and Floaties party, and Kappa Alpha's Beach Party and Dirty South.

The fraternity parties are open to all students who want to come. Non-Greek students, or even students from competing fraternities, are welcome. The only closed parties are fraternity-sorority mixers. W&L's administration is cracking down on fraternities for various violations: within the past few years, one was suspended and another was kicked off indefinitely. Most recently, there have been rumblings about the administration enforcing the University's official alcohol policy and stopping underage drinking at fraternity parties.

The College Prowler® Grade on
Greek Life: A+

A high grade in Greek Life indicates that sororities and fraternities are not only present, but also active on campus. Other determining factors include the variety of houses available and the respect the Greek community receives from the rest of the campus.

Drug Scene

The Lowdown On...
Drug Scene

Most Popular Drugs
Adderall
Alcohol
Marijuana
Nicotine

Alcohol-Related Referrals
56

Alcohol-Related Arrests
0

Drug-Related Referrals
14

Drug-Related Arrests
0

Drug Counseling Programs
Student Health Center
(540) 458-8401
Free counseling for depression and drug and alcohol dependency, referrals to specialists

University Counseling Program
(540) 458-8590
Confidential appointments with a licensed psychologist or psychiatrist

Students Speak Out On...
Drug Scene

Q Drugs and Alcohol
Hard drugs are present at W&L though more secluded than out in the open. Alcohol is simply a fact of life down here. It will be at every party you attend and in all of the fraternity houses. The only place where alcohol is present is the freshman dorms; RAs will crack down hard on it.

Q Several of my sorority sisters did not drink at the beginning of the year, some of them for moral reasons. Now I am the only member of my pledge class who does not drink. While I have never felt directly pressured to drink, W&L's social scene largely revolves around alcohol. I think that many students are indirectly pressured to drink.

Q Alcohol is easier to find than water at a frat party. Marijuana is pretty easy, too, assuming you know who to ask.

Q Drug use is very prevalent, especially the use of marijuana. It's kept pretty undercover, and there's certainly no pressure to use drugs, but a lot of students do, and it's easy to get drugs if you want them. Students rarely get caught, though.

Q Up until this year, I didn't drink. Even if you go out, I don't think there's a negative attitude towards people who don't drink. I've seen frat brothers ask people who don't drink if they'd like water or soda.

Q Compared to a state school, W&L's drug usage is pretty small. But alcohol is another story.

Q Caffeine is definitely seen in large quantities, and it seems like more people are smoking cigarettes.

Q Drug abuse seems prevalent around campus, in the sense that if you want drugs, you can probably find them. But it isn't obvious or being passed around the basement of a frat party.

The College Prowler Take On...
Drug Scene

Some of the information about the presence of drugs around campus is anecdotal and gossipy—not cold, hard facts. Marijuana use does occur, although it is mostly done off campus where houses aren't patrolled by security guards (as the freshman dorms and fraternities are). Washington and Lee students are less likely than their peers at 73 comparison schools to entirely avoid alcohol, cigarettes, and marijuana, according to the National College Health Assessment survey a few years ago. Compared to the reference group, W&L students report slightly higher rates of occasional cigarette and marijuana use, but average usage of harder drugs. Over 90 percent of students say they've never used harder drugs like cocaine or ecstasy. Investigators with the regional drug task force say they suspect marijuana use on campus but can't usually prove it. People tend to smoke cigarettes more at parties than for everyday use. Tobacco users that do not smoke usually use dipping or chewing tobacco.

Alcohol is the drug of choice at W&L, and is extremely prevalent both on and off campus. Knowing this, the University is trying to prevent drunk driving by providing free rides from parties back to campus. Students very rarely use fake IDs to get alcohol in Lexington, because the Executive Committee may consider it an honor violation and also because there's no point: on at least four nights out of the week, several fraternities will be holding open parties. Students frequently consume energy drinks due to the rigorous academic schedule, and do not be surprised to hear of some students using Adderall closer to midterms and finals.

The College Prowler® Grade on
Drug Scene: B

A high grade in the Drug Scene indicates that drugs are not a noticeable part of campus life; drug use is not visible, and no pressure to use them seems to exist.

Campus Strictness

The Lowdown On...
Campus Strictness

Students Are Most Likely to Get Caught...
Breaking the University's alcohol policies
Failing to register a vehicle.
Making excessive noise, but students can get away with quite a bit of rowdiness in the dorms.
Plagiarizing online materials
Trying to circumvent the school's policy against P2P downloading.
Unauthorized parking (see Parking section).

Did You Know?

W&L has a ton of student governance, and for a majority of the things that people get in trouble doing, the sanctions are handled by their peers, resulting in fair punishments. However, if one feels a sanction is too harsh, they are free to appeal it.

Students Speak Out On...
Campus Strictness

Q At times W&L is eerily reminiscent of a womb when compared to the realities of the outside world. The emergency blue-light stations that are so prominent on most campuses are virtually nonexistent here. Safety isn't even a concern because it is completely taken for granted.

Q Whether W&L security guards are strict or lenient depends on the situation. If you're caught drinking in the dorms or smoking pot, expect to be turned in for a strike. If you're caught illegally parking, you may be able to talk your way out of the ticket.

Q You get a 'strike' for drinking on campus if you're underage. One strike, and you get a letter sent to your parents, you're on probation for a year, and you have to talk to the Dean of Students. Two strikes within a one-year period and you're suspended (or can withdraw for a term). Third strike, you're out.

Q At worst, your car will get towed ($70 fee), and you'll get ticketed ($25) for parking violations. If you deface the dorms, or something like that, you may get a strike, depending upon the severity.

Q There is a low tolerance on drugs and a less than zero tolerance on drunk driving. This is the only place I know where a student can be expelled from school while arrested for drunk driving at home over break.

Q Strictness hasn't really hurt the social scene. The W&L social scene is still very vibrant. An administration paranoid about liability has done far more to damage it than any righteous group of badges ever could.

Q Underage drinking is a pasttime at W&L. It's generally tolerated. However, transporting alcohol back to the dormitories or drinking in your rooms can get you in trouble. Keep it to off-campus houses and fraternity parties and there will not be a problem.

Q Don't transport alcohol from party to party; it can only lead to hassle, and the party you're going to will almost certainly be well-stocked.

The College Prowler Take On...
Campus Strictness

Lexington falls under the jurisdiction of three police forces: the Lexington Police department, the Rockbridge County Sheriff's department, and the Virginia State Police. Police are serious about the speed limit, litter, noise, and public drunkenness and have no qualms about writing up students for any type of violation. Students who overstay their two-hour (or 15-minute) welcome in downtown parking spots are likely to be ticketed or have their cars towed. The good news is that W&L security guards tend to look the other way if students park at the curb and leave their blinkers on for a while.

If students are caught with alcohol in the dorms, they could be given a "strike"—three strikes within one year equals expulsion. Of course, the University in many ways has had a lenient attitude towards students. Smoking was allowed in freshman dorm rooms until the fall of 2004, and underage drinking went on all the time at fraternities, which are University property. But that laxness may be changing. Smoking is now prohibited in all undergraduate residence halls, and administrators made clear that they would get serious about enforcing the official regulations against underage drinking, effective immediately. The University has also begun cracking down on fraternities for any type of violation. Some students feel that it is becoming clear that the University is attempting to get rid of the prominent Greek life that Washington and Lee is known for.

The College Prowler® Grade on
Campus Strictness: C

A high Campus Strictness grade implies an overall lenient atmosphere; police and RAs are fairly tolerant, and the administration's rules are flexible.

Parking

The Lowdown On...
Parking

Parking Services
University Security and
Campus Services
(540) 458-8427
campuslife.wlu.edu/security

Approximate Parking Permit Cost
$50 per year

Student Parking Lot
Yes

Freshmen Allowed to Park
Yes

Common Parking Tickets

Expired time limit: $25
Fire lane: $25, plus $70 towing and $25 daily storage fee
Handicapped zone: $100, plus $70 towing and $25 daily storage fee
No parking zone: $25, plus $70 towing and $25 daily storage fee
Unauthorized parking in garage: $25, plus $70 towing and $25 daily storage fee

Getting a Parking Permit

Although the security office tries to discourage freshmen from bringing cars to campus, permits are available for the asking (and a $50 fee). Incoming freshmen are mailed a parking registration form in the summer before matriculation, however, they cannot park in town for more than two hours. W&L Security tows their cars after this, even if they are in 12-hour or unlimited-time spots.

Did You Know?

Best Places to Find a Parking Spot
For freshmen, there are no safe alternatives except the outdoor lot on the fringe of campus. For upperclassmen, the covered parking garage is prime real estate.

Good Luck Getting a Parking Spot Here! Washington Street between the front lawn and Early-Fielding Center. The two-hour spots are convenient—and coveted.

Students Speak Out On...
Parking

Q Awful Parking
Freshmen parking is horrendous as you must park in a lot one mile from the dorms. You cannot park in town or else the town will tow your car. Sophomore year, you park at the frats or srats with much more convenient access to your car.

Q Park where your permit allows you. I was towed almost 10 times my freshman year because I couldn't get that through my head.

Q Parking, unfortunately, is a huge problem here. We only have one actual parking garage, and you can get a permit for it depending upon where you live, but when people without permits park in the garage, it causes a big problem.

Q Security frequently tows permit-less parkers, but we need more parking, plain and simple, especially because almost every student has a car. And most of those cars are SUVs, by the way. If you're into conformity, bring an SUV.

Q Parking has always been a bit of a problem in Lexington, but the addition of the parking garage a few years back has greatly reduced this problem. As freshmen, not many people have a car and you don't really need one. After that, you do. If you're an upperclassman and live in town, security will usually help you: I live in downtown Lexington and was given a parking sticker for nearby fraternity lots.

Q No, it's not impossible to find a parking spot. But it's really easy to get a parking ticket, and the cops are really insane—they make it their job to give out tickets.

Q Don't bring a car as a freshman. The parking lot is really far and you'll just end up driving everyone around if you pledge a frat.

Q The parking deck is short walk from campus, but it's only for juniors, seniors, and sophomores living in dorms. The freshman parking lot is a five- to ten-minute walk from the main part of campus but not overly inconvenient.

The College Prowler Take On...
Parking

Three words: not so good. W&L freshmen have to park in an outdoor lot about half a mile from the dorms, which can be a major pain in bad weather. There is a large, four-story parking garage for students living in Gaines or the Woods Creek apartments (students who live a set distance away from campus can also use it). But construction has torn up outdoor lots close to Gaines and the Woods Creek apartments, pushing more cars into the covered garage, which is now at 100 percent capacity from mid-morning until after lunch. Moral of the story: students who are late to class may have to grab a parking spot in town.

Lexington, mercifully, does not have metered parking. Most parking spots off campus have two-hour limits, although some go for 12 hours. Students can theoretically park indefinitely on some side streets further from campus, but local homeowners might get nervous seeing an unknown car parked near their front porch. There are those students who take the risk to park illegally, both on and off campus, but as discussed earlier, they are usually risking a ticket and a towing bill.

The College Prowler® Grade on
Parking: C

A high grade in the Parking section indicates that parking is both available and affordable, and that parking enforcement isn't overly severe.

Transportation

The Lowdown On...
Transportation

Best Ways to Get Around Town
Borrow a friend's car
Ride a bike
Use your own car
Walk or jog

Public Transit
The Metrolink and Metrobus
(314) 231-2345
www.metrostlouis.org
An above-ground metro that runs to most key locations in the downtown area, and to Lambert International Airport, but not much else. Regular tickets cost $1.65, and the Metrolink runs until around 1:30 a.m. on weeknights, and 1 a.m. on weekends. The Metrobus runs throughout St. Louis and accepts the same tickets as Metrolink.

Best Ways to Get to the Airport
A cab ride to the airport costs around $60.
From Lexington, take I-81

South to Exit 143 onto Interstate 581/220 South. Take Exit 3E, Hershberger Road. Move over into the far left lane. Take the Aviation Drive/Airport exit. Move over into the far left lane. The airport terminal entrance is the second left.

Nearest Airport
Roanoke Regional Airport
(540) 362-1999
The airport is 45 miles and approximately 40 minutes from Washington and Lee.

Nearest Passenger Bus
Greyhound
211 W 21st St., Buena Vista
(800) 231-2222
www.greyhound.com
The Greyhound stop is in Buena Vista, approximately seven miles from campus.

Nearest Passenger Train
Amtrak
400 Ridgeway St., Clifton Forge
(800) 872-7245
www.amtrak.com
The closest Amtrak station is located approximately twenty miles away in Clifton Forge.

Students Speak Out On...
Transportation

Q There are a few local taxi services that offer cheap fares if you're desperate, but you can usually get a ride from a sober driver or a friend if you need one.

Q I have survived four years without a car, but occasionally you have to get creative when you need groceries or need to get away. There are two taxi services in town that have spotty reliability, but they are rather cheap. It would be better to have a car.

Q As for transportation to campus, you only need this if you live out in the country. Everywhere in town is pretty much walking or biking distance. You will need a car as an upperclassman living outside of town, and you will be allowed to park in the parking deck, a short walk from your first class.

Q W&L has a much-improved service known as Traveler, and although you may have to wait for a few minutes at a country party, Traveler has become quite reliable in my tenure here.

Q Traveler is a really great system that has mini-buses driving a route around campus and to off-campus student housing. There is also a car service that will pick you up anywhere, and campus security will come pick girls up if they are stranded somewhere.

Q What's annoying about the Traveler buses is that if you get on at a bad part of the route, you might be on the bus for half an hour.

Q Before the rule enforcement against underage drinking, Traveler was extensive enough. I think they're going to have to expand it a lot to fully accommodate students, because parties are going to be moved out to the country.

Q Town is within walking distance, so it's not a problem. Getting to Wal-Mart or Kroger is harder, but most students have cars, and now the university offers a weekend shuttle to Wal-Mart.

The College Prowler Take On...
Transportation

A car makes life at W&L a whole lot easier. Because Lexington is such a small town and many restaurants, stores, and parties are within walking distance, students can get by without one. Hitching rides with friends for trips to Wal-Mart or Roanoke is probably the most common way to get around. But a car brings the wider world closer, which is extremely valuable when you're in, well, such a small town. Its particularly necessary for the upperclassmen, since most live outside of town, though investing in a bike is also a good way to get from point A to point B.

In 2003, W&L introduced Traveler, a sober-drive shuttle service that takes students from campus to parties and back again until 2 a.m. on Monday, Wednesday, Friday, and Saturday nights. Before the program got off the ground, some alumni were concerned that the school was making it easier for students to get to off-campus drinking parties. But Traveler seems to be doing well in preventing drunk driving and getting students home safely. Now, drivers just have to focus on being on time. There are new concerns that the recent campus strictness may cause parties to move even further off campus outside of Traveler's route, which was recently limited to a five-mile radius. This could lead to potential problems with students getting stranded or driving drunk.

The College Prowler® Grade on Transportation: C+

A high grade for Transportation indicates that campus buses, public buses, cabs, and rental cars are readily-available and affordable. Other determining factors include proximity to an airport and the necessity of transportation.

Weather

The Lowdown On...
Weather

Temperature Averages
Spring – High: 67 °F
Spring – Low: 39 °F
Summer – High: 85 °F
Summer – Low: 60 °F
Fall – High: 69 °F
Fall – Low: 42 °F
Winter – High: 47 °F
Winter – Low: 23 °F

Precipitation Averages
Spring: 3.55 in.
Summer: 3.67 in.
Fall: 3.20 in.
Winter: 2.90 in.

Students Speak Out On...
Weather

Q So-So
Weather in the fall is beautiful. During winter, sleet and rain may occur one day, then it will be sunny and then there will be a terrible mix of cold and sun until March when everything warms up again.

Q Should you be in Lexington in the summer, expect it to be hot and, more importantly, humid. If you can arrange air-conditioning, I would highly recommend it.

Q There are four seasons in Lexington, although they all have their pitfalls. The summer is quite hot and humid. Fall tends to be pleasantly warm, although cold rains sometimes spoil things. Winters are mild, and most snow tends to fall while class is out of session for winter break. The weather is often mercurial and can change multiple times in one day.

Q Since a good many students live on or near campus, W&L never (barring a major weather-related disaster) cancels classes. This can pose a problem for students that live further away, in the more rural parts of the county, if they have to come to class on a particularly snowy day.

Q School never closes for the weather. All sophomores and freshmen live on campus but it can be difficult for upperclassmen living off campus, to make it safely to school when it's snowy or icy.

Q Bring clothes for all seasons. Obviously, winters aren't as bad as ones further north, but definitely bring hats, gloves, jackets, fleeces, and boots. Rain gear is a must.

Q Lexington is gorgeous during the summer. It is warm and sunny, though it does typically rain every day around 5 p.m. for about twenty minutes—honestly. Keep an umbrella with you during the summer.

Q Students often get depressed in winter because the weather and the workload are horrible. It's a very popular time to go abroad. I went to Australia winter term my junior year, and let's just say I didn't miss Lexington one little bit.

The College Prowler Take On...
Weather

The weather at Washington and Lee, true to form, varies wildly between steamy humidity, blue-sky glory, and frigid nastiness. There are four distinct seasons: hot and muggy in the early fall, crisp and nippy around Halloween, bitterly cold at Christmas time, and absolutely beautiful in the spring. Of course, the weather sometimes throws curveballs, and students have to be prepared. During the winter, moods tend to take a turn for the worse; a combination of the graying weather and heavier courseloads is enough to get even the most cheerful students down. For those that stick around during the summer time, be prepared to sweat it out, literally; summers are hot and humid, and air-conditioning becomes a necessity.

Some things never change: the freshman dorms at W&L still don't have air conditioning, so students either swelter through their first few weeks or buy a fan. Definitely choose the latter option. But it's important to remember that the early school year heat doesn't last for too long. The best thing to do is come prepared for all sorts of weather, or make sure to grab winter gear during Thanksgiving break. What makes up for the hot summer and long winter would be spring. During the spring, the weather is gorgeous, and there is a plethora of outdoor activities to keep students occupied.

The College Prowler® Grade on
Weather: C+

A high Weather grade designates that temperatures are mild and rarely reach extremes, that the campus tends to be sunny rather than rainy, and that weather is fairly consistent rather than unpredictable.

WASHINGTON & LEE UNIVERSITY
Report Card Summary

A ACADEMICS	**B** GUYS
C- LOCAL ATMOSPHERE	**B+** GIRLS
A HEALTH & SAFETY	**C+** ATHLETICS
A- COMPUTERS	**C-** NIGHTLIFE
B+ FACILITIES	**A+** GREEK LIFE
B CAMPUS DINING	**B** DRUG SCENE
B+ OFF-CAMPUS DINING	**C** CAMPUS STRICTNESS
B CAMPUS HOUSING	**C** PARKING
A- OFF-CAMPUS HOUSING	**C+** TRANSPORTATION
D DIVERSITY	**C+** WEATHER

Overall Experience

Students Speak Out On...
Overall Experience

💬 The Optimal College Experience
Perhaps W&L has the best blend of academics and fun in the United States. Professors will challenge you and expect you to work much harder than your peers that attend state schools. However, they are there to help you at any step of the learning process. Aside from academics, you can take part in the amazing greek system or the hundreds of outdoor adventure activities occuring every semester. W&L is definitely not for everyone. If you enjoy hiding or being anti-social and not taking advantage of your surroundings, then this place might not be for you. However, if you are outgoing, willing to talk to everyone and want to live in one America's most beautiful campus and setting for four years, then take W&L for the ride of your life.

Q W&L is not high school, and anyone entering as a freshman should expect to struggle somewhat integrating themselves into campus during their first year. Also, the academic expectations are much higher than those of a public high school. Almost every W&L students have the experience of receiving a bad mark on their first paper. This difficulty in adjusting, though, does pass, and eventually, people find ways of fitting in here.

Q W&L has an unfortunate reputation as a hard-partying and hard-drinking school. And to an extent, this is true. Anyone who ignores the University because of this does himself or herself a great disservice. Academics are exceedingly important at W&L, and the courses are typically very tough. Partying is important, but it never eclipses the more important reasons for being here for most students.

Q I knew that I wanted to come to W&L from the second I drove up, and it's met every single expectation that I had. The Honor Code is everything I expected, and the profs were more challenging—and yet more genuine—than I expected.

Q W&L is not for everybody. I've ended up really liking it because I've found people who share my interests. But then there's some people that the school's just not suited for. Make sure you look into the school extensively—spend the night if you can. Know that it's almost exclusively Greek—you have to be a really independent person to thrive here and enjoy it if you're not going to get involved in the Greek system.

Q I love W&L, but there are certain things about it that you need to like if you're going to enjoy yourself. First, you have to be cool about being at a really small school. You have to be comfortable enough with yourself if you're not from the South. Second, you should probably be okay with being in the Greek scene. Also, we don't inflate grades here. Yeah, you might be really smart, but it won't be easy. It's well known that certain teachers hate on freshmen.

Q I know that a W&L education means a lot—the alumni network is ridiculously good. The fact that you survived is cool enough. Let's not talk about graduating, because I love it so much. I'm actually contemplating going into law school here because I love it so much.

Q Sometimes, the stigma on W&L is that our students are too elitist or too Southern. I'll be honest—I see a lot of people on campus who think they're the most important people in the world. It's kind of annoying, really. But on the whole, W&L students are extremely kind, down to earth, generous people who, at the end of the day, don't give a damn about what kind of car you drive or where you went to prep school. They just want to know you. At least that's the case with the people I associate with.

The College Prowler Take On...
Overall Experience

Year after year, Washington and Lee has been remarkably successful at producing happy students. Freshmen usually come in starry-eyed, and leave four years later, content, happy, grateful for an awesome experience, and nostalgic for all the good times gone by. The demanding expectations of faculty don't seem to put a serious damper on the general feeling of good cheer. One objective gauge of this is W&L's remarkably active and supportive alumni network, which supports the University, stays in touch to get jobs for students, and most recently, chipped in cash to the tune of $240 million for massive modernization projects.

Students give high marks to the educational quality here, as well as to the natural setting and the sense of community and respect engendered by the Honor System and a tradition of gentility. But as their comments have shown, some students are put off by the small-town environment and the dominance of Greek life on campus, as well as by recent friction between students and the administration over alcohol policies and changes to their beloved Spring term. Most biting is some of the criticism leveled at the Greek system for allegedly crippling the social options for students who don't really want to party all the time. Many students here believe their school is like no other—an example of what college life should be—and want to keep it that way.

The Inside Scoop

The Lowdown On...
The Inside Scoop

School Slang
The Administration: Generally the University's policymakers—the President, deans, and trustees.
Ball: To blackball, or deny membership to a fraternity or sorority.
BDG quad: Courtyard of the Baker-Davis-Gilliam dorm complex.
BV: Buena Vista, a nearby town.
Cadaver: A member of a W&L secret society known for donating large amounts of money and running around in masks.
Co-op: Upperclassman slang (rapidly disappearing) for the Café.
C-School: Williams School of Commerce, Economics, and Politics.

Davidson Park: The eight fraternities located between East Nelson and East Washington streets.

D-Hall: The Marketplace, or "dining hall."

East Lex: General store and "beverage" outlet on the outskirts of town.

EC: Student Executive Committee. Elected representatives that administer the honor system and oversee student organizations.

FD: Fancy Dress Ball, the biggest party at W&L every year. Cocktail dresses and tuxes—the whole nine yards.

Foxfield: Biannual horse race in Charlottesville; pack sunscreen.

GAB: General Activities Board, a student organization that sponsors entertainment like hypnotists and illusionists, comedians, and bands.

Goshen: The local area's little piece of heaven. Roadside stop-offs are favorite spots for grilling, sunbathing, and swimming.

The Hill: Main campus (the part with academic buildings).

HV: Honor violation (decided by the EC in cases involving dishonorable conduct, usually lying, cheating, or stealing).

J-School: Journalism School, housed in Reid Hall.

The Phi: The Ring Tum Phi, W&L's oldest student newspaper.

Red Square: The five Fraternities across from the Corral.

The Ruins: All that's left of Liberty Hall, W&L's first incarnation. Located near the freshman parking lot.

SJC: Student Judicial Council, student government body (elected student representatives) that enforces the University's policies on drugs and alcohol.

State: The State Theater, the Nelson Street movie house.

Stop-In: Gas station and convenience store near Lee Chapel, famous for late-night snack runs.

Townie: A non-W&L student who lives in Lexington or the surrounding Rockbridge County.

Veemie: A VMI cadet.

Things I Wish I Knew Before Coming To School

- Get to the dorm room early and grab the bottom bunk.
- How big the frat scene is.
- How much fun studying abroad is.

- How to do laundry (whites do not go in the washer with reds).
- How to do navigate a big library and write a college-level research paper.
- How tough the work is.
- How useful a laptop is on a beautiful day.
- The mini-fridge is not very useful—and is nasty to clean out.
- The science majors have a ghastly amount of studying.
- What all the Greek letters meant.

Tips to Succeed

- Do the reading, and don't fall behind.
- Don't cheat—it's not worth it.
- Don't join a frat or sorority just because "everyone else is doing it;" decide for yourself.
- Even if you're a studyholic, take time to visit Goshen or play Frisbee on the front lawn.
- Go to class—if you don't, it will catch up with you.
- Introduce yourself to people in your dorm.
- Keep an open mind about your future major.
- Keep in touch with friends from freshman year.
- Meet the security staff.
- Put hard and fast limits on your drinking—and drink responsibly.
- Shower before class.
- Talk to your professors if you don't understand something.
- Try to get a good internship.

Traditions

Christmas Concerts in Lee Chapel : A better use of W&L's historic landmarks. The concert brings the Lexington community and W&L's singers together for a night of peace, beautiful music, and Christmas good cheer.

Dinner with the President : Every graduating senior joins a small group of his or her classmates for dinner in the Lee House with the University President and his wife. Stimulating conversation and excellent food are the order of the day. Make sure the hosts tell you about Robert E. Lee's stay in the house. Note: check out the ivory carvings and various treasures, but do not drop anything. Major faux pas.

Fancy Dress: The annual bash that defines "party" at W&L. The Warner Center basketball courts and the Doremus Gym are transformed into huge themed dance halls for the $80,000 event. Recent themes include Bond, James Bond—"Dressed to Kill: Always Shakin' Never Stirred" — for the 96th annual FD, and Willy Wonka and the Chocolate Factory for the 97th.

Hiking House Mountain: Everybody here feels guilty if they don't climb Lexington's most prominent mountain at least once before graduation. The views of the countryside are amazing (or so they say—a certain writer still needs to get off the couch and try it).

Mock Convention : Or, if peace isn't really your thing, try some rip-roarin' politics on for size. "Mock Con" is the biggest thing to hit Lexington every four years—a student-run convention organized just like a real presidential convention. Running since 1908, Mock Con has a near-perfect record since 1948 (it's been wrong once) at correctly predicting the presidential candidate for the challenging party. Take that, exit polls! Over 90 percent of students participate in the event, which has drawn speakers including, James Carville, Al Sharpton, Bob Dole, Jimmy Carter, and Harry Truman.

Speaking Tradition : The long-standing rule at W&L was that you would exchange a hearty greeting with anyone who crossed your path—professor, student, or townie. (Some freshman hell-raisers were allegedly whacked with canes in the early 20th century when upperclassmen caught them neglecting the tradition.) This tradition still persists (the speaking, not the beating), but it seems to be hanging by a thread. Upperclassmen blame freshmen for ignoring the traditions of courtesy, but everybody needs to do their part.

Spring Term: Students revere the six-week term for the glorious weather, slightly more relaxed classes, and the opportunities it creates for international travel and study. Frisbee, tubing, and sunbathing—much of it away from campus, at Goshen—abound. The unusual schedule gives professors a short period in which they can teach hybrid courses (see the Washington Term Program) or study a focused topic in-depth ("Violence in the South" in the English Department, "Enron and Martha Stewart" in the Journalism

Department, and so on). However, not all is rosy. Strains on professors, the need to cut costs, and the perception that students take it too easy during the term led the Board of Trustees to cut back Spring Term in February 2004—students will only be able to participate for three of their four years here, starting in 2007.

Streaking on the Colonnade: And you thought only British soccer fans ran naked. Streaking down the walkway of the historic academic buildings on the front campus is a W&L tradition as old as, well, we don't really know, but it shows no signs of stopping. The purpose: unclear. The subjects: typically frat pledges, but may include groups of inebriated coeds.

Vanished Traditions : Unfortunately, some traditions are unmistakably vanishing at W&L. Students used to scurry, Catacombs-style, through underground pipes that run beneath the campus, but no longer—the gates are locked shut. We used to carve initials into the tables at the Spanky's sandwich joint, but no longer—the old place is closed. What's next, I ask you?

Urban Legends

- Traveler, Robert E. Lee's prized thoroughbred, haunts the streets of Lexington. The President of W&L has to leave his garage door open so that the horse can go in and out of what was once his stable. Sometime in the 1930s, W&L frat boys—Sigma Nu gentlemen, it is said—strapped on Tommie guns, Al Capone-style, and commandeered a train to bring their dates from Hollins University back to campus. If it rains on freshman move-in day, it will be sunny and beautiful on graduation day. The student lucky enough to catch, unmask, and identify a member of the elusive Cadaver Society will be set up with full payment of medical school bills. Good luck.

Students Speak Out On...
The Inside Scoop

💬 Career Services
W&L Career Services is one of our greatest assets. Through alumni and personal connections and a good GPA, they can place you in internships - which the school can subsidize - which will eventually land you a sweet job.

Jobs & Internships

The Lowdown On...
Jobs & Internships

Career Center
John W. Elrod University Commons 301
(540) 458-8595 (540) 458-8097 (fax)
careers@wlu.edu
careers.wlu.edu

Employment Services?
No

Placement Services?
Yes

Other Career Services
Colonnade Connections national electronic alumni network.
eRecruiting
Job and internship directories
On-campus recruiting and off-campus interviewing days
Personal career counseling.
Practice interviews, professional résumé critiques.
Specialized career workshops for liberal arts majors, public sector employment.

Advice

On average, it probably takes more effort for a W&L student to get a sweet job or internship than it does for a student at a bigger school, just because some recruiters ignore small-town schools. But the University and its very generous and well-connected alumni provide a wealth of resources to help students get out into the real world. In the Career Services office, students can search huge databases of internships and jobs, go over their resumé and cover letters with a professional job coordinator, and groom themselves for the big meeting with practice interviews.   The University has joined numerous job-bank programs to compensate for the fact that many employers don't recruit in Lexington. Many of these programs are aimed specifically at liberal arts majors—say, English and history majors—who might otherwise have a lot of trouble finding paying jobs. But be warned: investment banking and consulting firms still seem to dominate the on-campus recruitment, so C-School majors (accounting, economics) still seem to have an advantage.   Start early, during freshman year if possible. Get to know the Career Services staff; they are very knowledgeable and can help you tailor your search to jobs and internships that fit your interest. Search the employment databases periodically, and write down application deadlines. Try to have a résumé handy, in case the ideal opportunity drops out a clear blue sky. After freshman year, use Colonnade Connections to find helpful alumni (but use tact and good etiquette in contacting them).

Firms That Most Frequently Hire Grads

AC Nielsen BASES
Accenture
Bank of America
Catlin Underwriting Agency U. S., Inc.
CLICKS
Design Cuisine
Ellis Commercial Real Estate
Ernst and Young, LLP
Fairfax County Schools
Hewitt Associates
Morgan Stanley

Peace Corps
Porzio, Bromberg, and Newman
Price Waterhouse Coopers
Reznick, Fedder, and Silverman
Wachovia Securities
Washington & Lee University

Did You Know?

Check out what Fortune said about W&L in June 1990. "When…schools' ability to graduate future CEOs is adjusted for class size, a few lesser-known institutions out-shine the giants. Relatively speaking, tiny Washington & Lee of Lexington, Virginia, has launched more alumni toward the corner office than mighty Harvard." The survey showed W&L just behind Yale and Princeton in the adjusted rankings.

From "Where the CEOs went to college:" a Fortune survey of the nation's top bosses shows that the Ivies and Big Ten schools rank high. But wait! Little Johnny or Janie may want to consider Washington & Lee." Susan Caminiti, Fortune, June 18, 1990.

Washington and Lee has produced four U.S. Supreme Court Justices, 27 U.S. Senators, 31 governors and 67 congressmen.

Alumni & Post-Grads

The Lowdown On...
Alumni & Post-Grads

Alumni Office
Alumni Office
Letcher Avenue, Lexington
Phone: (540) 458-8464
Fax: (540) 458-8473
alumni.wlu.edu

Major Alumni Events
The biggest events for alumni every year are Homecoming, which features raucous football games (plus a hearty tailgate lunch), crazy parties, and plenty of reminiscing; and Reunion, where the graduate class with the best attendance wins the Reunion Bowl.

There is also Alumni College—alums can either go abroad on trips to places like France or the Galapagos Islands or come to campus for a combination of vacation and study on the Civil War, the historical Jesus, and Tom Wolfe's Bonfire of the Vanities.

Services Available

Colonnade Connections (helps alums track down buddies), transcript/diploma mailings, local chapter gatherings (some complete with a cappella concerts), Alumni House wining and dining on special weekends.

Alumni Publications

W&L, the Washington and Lee University alumni magazine. This free quarterly magazine features a variety of articles on current students, happenings at the University, and faculty. It reaches about 30,000 alumni, parents, and friends of the University.

Did You Know?

Famous W&L Alumni

David Brown (Class of 2000) – Host and senior editor, NPR's "Marketplace" business news show.

Meriwether Clark (Class of 1790) – Secretary to Thomas Jefferson, co-leader of the Lewis and Clark expedition, and Governor of Louisiana Territory.

Roger H. Mudd (Class of 1950) – Congressional correspondent (CBS, PBS) and History Channel host.

Lewis F. Powell Jr. (Class of 1929) – Associate justice on the US Supreme Court and president of the American Bar Association.

Pat Robertson (Class of 1950) – Chancellor of Regent University and founder of the Christian Broadcasting Network and the Christian Coalition.

John Warner (Class of 1949) – U.S. senator and Secretary of the Navy.

Tom Wolfe (Class of 1951) – Bestselling author of Bonfire of the Vanities, A Man in Full, and I Am Charlotte Simmons.

Student Organizations

The Lowdown On...

ROTC
Air Force ROTC: No
Navy ROTC: No
Army ROTC: Yes

Student Activities Offered

Alpha Phi Omega
Ariel
Baptist Student Union
Bonner Leaders
Cable Channel 2
Calyx
Canterbury Club
Catholic Campus Ministry
Club Asia
College Libertarians
College Republicans
Committee for the Charity Ball benefiting Cystic Fibrosis
Community Service
Concert Guild
Contact Committee
Ducks Unlimited
Eastern Orthodox Campus Ministry
English for Speakers of
Executive Committee of the Student Body (EC)
Fancy Dress Committee
Film Society
Freshman Leadership Council (FLC)
Freshmen Orientation Committee (FOC)
Gay-Straight Alliance
General Activities Board (GAD)
General Admission
General and Academic
Generals' Christian Fellowship
Good Shepherd Lutheran
Habitat for Humanity
Hillel
inGeneral
Interfraternity Council (IFC)
International House
Journal of Science
Joyful Noise gospel choir
JubiLee
Kathekon
Knowledge Empowering Women Leaders (KEWL)
Liberty Hall Volunteers
Lifestyle Information for Everyone (LIFE)
Mindbending Productions
Minority Student Association (MSA)
Mock Convention
Mock Trial
Muslim League
Nabors Service League
Nicaragua Project
One in Four
Onyx
Order of Omega
Other Languages
Outing Club
Panhellenic Council
Peer Counselors
Performing Arts
Phi Eta Sigma
Photography Club
Politically Charged
Politics
Programming
Programming for the
Publications
Reformed University Fellowship
Religion
Respect of Individuals and Diversity in Education

The Ring-tum Phi
SAIL International Development and Relief Group (IDRG)
SAIL International Student Alliance
SAIL Model United Nations (MUN)
SAIL Outreach Committee
Society of Thought
Southern Comfort
Spanish House
Student Activities Organization (SAO)
Student Association for International Learning (SAIL)
Student Government
Student Judicial Council (SJC)
Student Recruitment Committee
Student-Faculty Hearing Board (SFHB)
Students Against Rockbridge Area Hunger (S.A.R.A.H.)
Theater Outreach
Traveler
The Trident
Trinity United Methodist
U.S. Army ROTC (hosted by VMI)
University Chamber Singers
University Chorus
University Jazz Ensemble
University Scholars
University Theatre
University Wind Ensemble
University-Shenandoah Symphony Orchestra
W&L Dance – Jazz and Tap
W&L Dance Ensemble
W&L March of Dimes Collegiate Council
W&L Political Review
W&L Students for Life
Washington and Lee Cheerleading
Washington and Lee Knitting Society
Washington and Lee NAACP College
Washington and Lee Student Consulting
Washington and Lee Turkish Generals
Williams Investment Society
WLUR 91.5 FM
Women in Technology and Science (WITS)
Women's Forum
Young Democrats
Young Life

The Best

The **BEST** Things

1. Academic excellence

2. Friendly, trusting, close-knit community

3. The Honor Code and being able to trust your classmates

4. Greek madness and the fun social scene

5. Beautiful campus and surrounding area

6. Small classes and personal attention from caring professors

7. The Commons

8. Wasting days looking people up on the Facebook

9. (Generally) cool alumni - good ol' boys mixed with up-and-comers

10. Leisurely pace of life in a small town

The Worst

The **WORST** Things

1. Waking up in a trashed and disgusting residence after a big party weekend

2. A sometimes tone-deaf administration

3. Lack of alternatives to Greek activities and partying

4. Seriously cramped parking

5. Slack support for Division III athletics - missing the "big sports" atmosphere

6. Greek madness and prevalence of alcohol

7. Lack of a city

8. Heavy academic demands

9. Little diversity

10. Not being able to pick up radio stations

Visiting

The Lowdown On...
Visiting

Campus Tours
Campus tours run Monday through Saturday, except on holidays, between semesters, and during finals. (Saturday tours are not available in the summer). Between September and December and during May, weekday tours depart every hour between 10 a.m. and 3 p.m. Morning tours are available between January and April. Check with the Admissions office for tour availability, and get to the Gilliam House (Admissions office) 10 minutes early! Most tours are guided by current W&L students.

Interviews & Information Sessions
Call the Admissions office at (540) 458-8710 on any weekday from 8:30 a.m.–4:30 p.m. EST. The Admissions staff interviews Mondays through Saturdays between May and December.

On-campus interviews are not offered December 17 through April 30, but students can interview off-campus with W&L alumni in their local area until January 31. Note: Washington and Lee "strongly recommends" that applicants have an interview.

Overnight Visits

Accepted students are invited to campus for overnight stays in the spring, and recruits for varsity sports also come to campus for hosted visits. Students competing for Honor Scholarships are required to make a two-day visit. Regular applicants do not usually stay overnight until accepted. Rising high school seniors can get the authentic W&L experience through the Summer Scholars program. About 150 students spend four weeks at W&L, living in the dorms, sampling the food, and studying real University courses (taught by real faculty) in journalism, business, pre-med studies, politics, or law. Check out the program at http://summerscholars.wlu.edu

Words to Know

Academic Probation – A suspension imposed on a student if he or she fails to keep up with the school's minimum academic requirements. Those unable to improve their grades after receiving this warning can face dismissal.

Beer Pong/Beirut – A drinking game involving cups of beer arranged in a pyramid shape on each side of a table. The goal is to get a ping pong ball into one of the opponent's cups by throwing the ball or hitting it with a paddle. If the ball lands in a cup, the opponent is required to drink the beer.

Bid – An invitation from a fraternity or sorority to 'pledge' (join) that specific house.

Blue-Light Phone – Brightly-colored phone posts with a blue light bulb on top. These phones exist for security purposes and are located at various outside locations around most campuses. In an emergency, a student can pick up one of these phones (free of charge) to connect with campus police or a security escort.

Campus Police – Police who are specifically assigned to a given institution. Campus police are typically not regular city officers; they are employed by the university in a full-time capacity.

Club Sports – A level of sports that falls somewhere between varsity and intramural. If a student is unable to commit to a varsity team but has a lot of passion for athletics, a club sport could be a better, less intense option. Even less demanding, intramural (IM) sports often involve no traveling and considerably less time.

Cocaine – An illegal drug. Also known as "coke" or "blow," cocaine often resembles a white crystalline or powdery substance. It is highly addictive and dangerous.

Common Application – An application with which students can apply to multiple schools.

Course Registration – The period of official class selection for the upcoming quarter or semester. Prior to registration, it is best to prepare several back-up courses in case a particular class becomes full. If a course is full, students can place themselves on the waitlist, although this still does not guarantee entry.

Division Athletics – Athletic classifications range from Division I to Division III. Division IA is the most competitive, while Division III is considered to be the least competitive.

Dorm – A dorm (or dormitory) is an on-campus housing facility. Dorms can provide a range of options from suite-style rooms to more communal options that include shared bathrooms. Most first-year students live in dorms. Some upperclassmen who wish to stay on campus also choose this option.

Early Action – An application option with which a student can apply to a school and receive an early acceptance response without a binding commitment. This system is becoming less and less available.

Early Decision – An application option that students should use only if they are certain they plan to attend the school in question. If a student applies using the early decision option and is admitted, he or she is required and bound to attend that university. Admission rates are usually higher among students who apply through early decision, as the student is clearly indicating that the school is his or her first choice.

Ecstasy – An illegal drug. Also known as "E" or "X," ecstasy looks like a pill and most resembles an aspirin. Considered a party drug, ecstasy is very dangerous and can be deadly.

Ethernet – An extremely fast Internet connection available in most university-owned residence halls. To use an Ethernet connection properly, a student will need a network card and cable for his or her computer.

Fake ID – A counterfeit identification card that contains false information. Most commonly, students get fake IDs with altered birthdates so that they appear to be older than 21 (and therefore of legal drinking age). Even though it is illegal, many college students have fake IDs in hopes of purchasing alcohol or getting into bars.

Frosh – Slang for "freshman" or "freshmen."

Hazing – Initiation rituals administered by some fraternities or sororities as part of the pledging process. Many universities have outlawed hazing due to its degrading, and sometimes dangerous, nature.

Intramurals (IMs) – A popular, and usually free, sport league in which students create teams and compete against one another. These sports vary in competitiveness and can include a range of activities—everything from billiards to water polo. IM sports are a great way to meet people with similar interests.

Keg – Officially called a half-barrel, a keg contains roughly 200 12-ounce servings of beer.

LSD – An illegal drug, also known as acid, this hallucinogenic drug most commonly resembles a tab of paper.

Marijuana – An illegal drug, also known as weed or pot; along with alcohol, marijuana is one of the most commonly found drugs on campuses across the country.

Major – The focal point of a student's college studies; a specific topic that is studied for a degree. Examples of majors include physics, English, history, computer science, economics, business, and music. Many students decide on a specific major before arriving on campus, while others are simply "undecided" until declaring a major. Those who are extremely interested in two areas can also choose to double major.

Meal Block – The equivalent of one meal. Students on a meal plan usually receive a fixed number of meals per week. Each meal, or "block," can be redeemed at the school's dining facilities in place of cash. Often, a student's weekly allotment of meal blocks will be forfeited if not used.

Minor – An additional focal point in a student's education. Often serving as a complement or addition to a student's main area of focus, a minor has fewer requirements and prerequisites to fulfill than a major. Minors are not required for graduation from most schools; however some students who want to explore many different interests choose to pursue both a major and a minor.

Mushrooms – An illegal drug. Also known as "'shrooms," this drug resembles regular mushrooms but is extremely hallucinogenic.

Off-Campus Housing – Housing from a particular landlord or rental group that is not affiliated with the university. Depending on the college, off-campus housing can range from extremely popular to non-existent. Students who choose to live off campus are typically given more freedom, but they also have to deal with possible subletting scenarios, furniture, bills, and other issues. In addition to these factors, rental prices and distance often affect a student's decision to move off campus.

Office Hours – Time that teachers set aside for students who have questions about coursework. Office hours are a good forum for students to go over any problems and to show interest in the subject material.

Pledging – The early phase of joining a fraternity or sorority, pledging takes place after a student has gone through rush and received a bid. Pledging usually lasts between one and two semesters. Once the pledging period is complete and a particular student has done everything that is required to become a member, that student is considered a brother or sister. If a fraternity or a sorority would decide to "haze" a group of students, this initiation would take place during the pledging period.

Private Institution – A school that does not use tax revenue to subsidize education costs. Private schools typically cost more than public schools and are usually smaller.

Prof – Slang for "professor."

Public Institution – A school that uses tax revenue to subsidize education costs. Public schools are often a good value for in-state residents and tend to be larger than most private colleges.

Quarter System (or Trimester System) – A type of academic calendar system. In this setup, students take classes for three academic periods. The first quarter usually starts in late September or early October and concludes right before Christmas. The second quarter usually starts around early to mid–January and finishes up around March or April. The last academic quarter, or "third quarter," usually starts in late March or early April and finishes up in late May or Mid-June. The fourth quarter is summer. The major difference between the quarter system and semester system is that students take more, less comprehensive courses under the quarter calendar.

RA (Resident Assistant) – A student leader who is assigned to a particular floor in a dormitory in order to help to the other students who live there. An RA's duties include ensuring student safety and providing assistance wherever possible.

Recitation – An extension of a specific course; a review session. Some classes, particularly large lectures, are supplemented with mandatory recitation sessions that provide a relatively personal class setting.

Rolling Admissions – A form of admissions. Most commonly found at public institutions, schools with this type of policy continue to accept students throughout the year until their class sizes are met. For example, some schools begin accepting students as early as December and will continue to do so until April or May.

Room and Board – This figure is typically the combined cost of a university-owned room and a meal plan.

Room Draw/Housing Lottery – A common way to pick on-campus room assignments for the following year. If a student decides to remain in university-owned housing, he or she is assigned a unique number that, along with seniority, is used to determine his or her housing for the next year.

Rush – The period in which students can meet the brothers and sisters of a particular chapter and find out if a given fraternity or sorority is right for them. Rushing a fraternity or a sorority is not a requirement at any school. The goal of rush is to give students who are serious about pledging a feel for what to expect.

Semester System – The most common type of academic calendar system at college campuses. This setup typically includes two semesters in a given school year. The fall semester starts around the end of August or early September and concludes before winter vacation. The spring semester usually starts in mid-January and ends in late April or May.

Student Center/Rec Center/Student Union – A common area on campus that often contains study areas, recreation facilities, and eateries. This building is often a good place to meet up with fellow students; depending on the school, the student center can have a huge role or a non-existent role in campus life.

Student ID – A university-issued photo ID that serves as a student's key to school-related functions. Some schools require students to show these cards in order to get into dorms, libraries, cafeterias, and other facilities. In addition to storing meal plan information, in some cases, a student ID can actually work as a debit card and allow students to purchase things from bookstores or local shops.

Suite – A type of dorm room. Unlike dorms that feature communal bathrooms shared by the entire floor, suites offer bathrooms shared only among the suite. Suite-style dorm rooms can house anywhere from two to ten students.

TA (Teacher's Assistant) – An undergraduate or grad student who helps in some manner with a specific course. In some cases, a TA will teach a class, assist a professor, grade assignments, or conduct office hours.

Undergraduate – A student in the process of studying for his or her bachelor's degree.

About the Author

Name: Zachary John Barbieri

Hometown: Wayne, NJ

Major: Accounting and Philosophy

Fun Fact: Zachary is the first person in his immediate family to attend college.

Previous Contributors: Jeremiah McWilliams

Pros and Cons

Still can't figure out if this is the right school for you? You've already read through this in-depth guide; why not list the pros and cons? It will really help with narrowing down your decision and determining whether or not this school is right for you.

Pros	**Cons**
....	....
....	....
....	....
....	....
....	....
....	....
....	....
....	....
....	....
....	....
....	....
....	....

Pros and Cons

Still can't figure out if this is the right school for you? You've already read through this in-depth guide; why not list the pros and cons? It will really help with narrowing down your decision and determining whether or not this school is right for you.

Pros	**Cons**
....	....
....	....
....	....
....	....
....	....
....	....
....	....
....	....
....	....
....	....
....	....
....	....

Notes

Notes

Notes

Notes

Notes

Notes

Notes

Notes

Notes

Notes

Notes

Notes

Notes

Notes

Notes

Notes

Notes

College Scholarships

Search. Apply. Win!

College Prowler gives away thousands of dollars each month through our popular monthly scholarships, including our $2,000 "No Essay" scholarship.

Plus, we'll connect you with hundreds of other scholarships based on your unique information and qualifications!

Create a College Prowler account today to get matched with millions of dollars in relevant scholarships!

**Sign up and apply now at
www.collegeprowler.com/register**

Review Your School!

Let your voice be heard.

Every year, thousands of students take our online survey to share their opinions about campus life.

Now's your chance to help millions of high school students choose the right college for them.

Tell us what life is really like at your school by taking our online survey or even uploading your own photos and videos!

And as our thanks to you for participating in our survey, we'll enter you into a random drawing for our $1,000 Monthly Survey Scholarship!

For more information, check out
www.collegeprowler.com/survey

Write For Us!

Express your opinion. Get published!

Interested in being a published author? College Prowler is always on the lookout for current college students across the country to write the guides for their schools.

The contributing author position is a unique opportunity for eager college students to bolster their résumés and portfolios, become published authors both online and in print, and gain tremendous exposure to millions of high school students nationwide.

For more details, visit
www.collegeprowler.com/careers

Order now! • collegeprowler.com • (800) 290-2682
More than 400 single-school guides available!

Albion College
Alfred University
Allegheny College
Alverno College
American Intercontinental University Online
American University
Amherst College
Arizona State University
Ashford University
The Art Institute of California – Orange County
Auburn University
Austin College
Babson College
Ball State University
Bard College
Barnard College
Barry University
Baruch College
Bates College
Bay Path College
Baylor University
Beloit College
Bentley University
Berea College
Binghamton University
Birmingham Southern College
Bob Jones University
Boston College
Boston University
Bowdoin College
Bradley University
Brandeis University
Brigham Young University
Brigham Young University – Idaho
Brown University
Bryant University
Bryn Mawr College
Bucknell University
Cal Poly Pomona
California College of the Arts
California Institute of Technology
California Polytechnic State University
California State University – Monterey Bay
California State University – Northridge
California State University – San Marcos
Carleton College
Carnegie Mellon University
Case Western Reserve University
Catawba College
Catholic University of America

Centenary College of Louisiana
Centre College
Chapman University
Chatham University
City College of New York
City College of San Francisco
Claflin University
Claremont McKenna College
Clark Atlanta University
Clark University
Clemson University
Cleveland State University
Colby College
Colgate University
College of Charleston
College of Mount Saint Vincent
College of Notre Dame of Maryland
College of the Holy Cross
College of William & Mary
College of Wooster
Colorado College
Columbia College Chicago
Columbia University
Concordia University – Wisconsin
Connecticut College
Contra Costa College
Cornell College
Cornell University
Creighton University
CUNY Lehman College
CUNY Queens College
CUNY Queensborough Community College
Dalton State College
Dartmouth College
Davidson College
De Anza College
Del Mar College
Denison University
DePaul University
DePauw University
Diablo Valley College
Dickinson College
Dordt College
Drexel University
Duke University
Duquesne University
Earlham College
East Carolina University
Eckerd College
El Paso Community College
Elon University
Emerson College
Emory University
Fashion Institute of Design & Merchandising

Fashion Institute of Technology
Ferris State University
Florida Atlantic University
Florida Southern College
Florida State University
Fordham University
Franklin & Marshall College
Franklin Pierce University
Frederick Community College
Freed-Hardeman University
Furman University
Gannon University
Geneva College
George Mason University
George Washington University
Georgetown University
Georgia Institute of Technology
Georgia Perimeter College
Georgia State University
Germanna Community College
Gettysburg College
Gonzaga University
Goucher College
Grinnell College
Grove City College
Guilford College
Gustavus Adolphus College
Hamilton College
Hampshire College
Hampton University
Hanover College
Harvard University
Harvey Mudd College
Hastings College
Haverford College
Hillsborough Community College
Hofstra University
Hollins University
Howard University
Hunter College (CUNY)
Idaho State University
Illinois State University
Illinois Wesleyan University
Indiana Univ.–Purdue Univ. Indianapolis (IUPUI)
Indiana University
Iowa State University
Ithaca College
Jackson State University
James Madison University
Johns Hopkins University
Juniata College
Kansas State University
Kaplan University

Kent State University
Kenyon College
La Roche College
Lafayette College
Lawrence University
Lehigh University
Lewis & Clark College
Linfield College
Los Angeles City College
Los Angeles Valley College
Louisiana College
Louisiana State University
Loyola College in Maryland
Loyola Marymount University
Loyola University Chicago
Luther College
Macalester College
Macomb Community College
Manhattan College
Manhattanville College
Marlboro College
Marquette University
Maryville University
Massachusetts College of Art & Design
Massachusetts Institute of Technology
McGill University
Merced College
Mercyhurst College
Messiah College
Miami University
Michigan State University
Middle Tennessee State University
Middlebury College
Millsaps College
Minnesota State University – Moorhead
Missouri State University
Montana State University
Montclair State University
Moorpark College
Mount Holyoke College
Muhlenberg College
New College of Florida
New York University
North Carolina A&T State University
North Carolina State University
Northeastern University
Northern Arizona University
Northern Illinois University
Northwest Florida State College
Northwestern College – Saint Paul
Northwestern University

- Oakwood University
- Oberlin College
- Occidental College
- Oglethorpe University
- Ohio State University
- Ohio University
- Ohio Wesleyan University
- Old Dominion University
- Onondaga Community College
- Oral Roberts University
- Pace University
- Palm Beach State College
- Penn State Altoona
- Penn State Brandywine
- Penn State University
- Pepperdine University
- Pitzer College
- Pomona College
- Princeton University
- Providence College
- Purdue University
- Radford University
- Ramapo College of New Jersey
- Reed College
- Rensselaer Polytechnic Institute
- Rhode Island School of Design
- Rhodes College
- Rice University
- Rider University
- Robert Morris University
- Rochester Institute of Technology
- Rocky Mountain College of Art & Design
- Rollins College
- Rowan University
- Rutgers University
- Sacramento State
- Saint Francis University
- Saint Joseph's University
- Saint Leo University
- Salem College
- Salisbury University
- Sam Houston State University
- Samford University
- San Diego State University
- San Francisco State University
- Santa Clara University
- Santa Fe College
- Sarah Lawrence College
- Scripps College
- Seattle University
- Seton Hall University
- Simmons College
- Skidmore College
- Slippery Rock University
- Smith College
- South Texas College
- Southern Methodist University
- Southwestern University
- Spelman College
- St. John's College – Annapolis
- St. John's University
- St. Louis University
- St. Mary's University
- St. Olaf College
- Stanford University
- State University of New York – Purchase College
- State University of New York at Fredonia
- State University of New York at Oswego
- Stetson University
- Stevens-Henager College
- Stony Brook University (SUNY)
- Susquehanna University
- Swarthmore College
- Syracuse University
- Taylor University
- Temple University
- Tennessee State University
- Texas A&M University
- Texas Christian University
- Texas Tech
- The Community College of Baltimore County
- Towson University
- Trinity College (Conn.)
- Trinity University (Texas)
- Troy University
- Truman State University
- Tufts University
- Tulane University
- Union College
- University at Albany (SUNY)
- University at Buffalo (SUNY)
- University of Alabama
- University of Arizona
- University of Arkansas
- University of Arkansas at Little Rock
- University of California – Berkeley
- University of California – Davis
- University of California – Irvine
- University of California – Los Angeles
- University of California – Merced
- University of California – Riverside
- University of California – San Diego
- University of California – Santa Barbara
- University of California – Santa Cruz
- University of Central Florida
- University of Chicago
- University of Cincinnati
- University of Colorado
- University of Connecticut
- University of Delaware
- University of Denver
- University of Florida
- University of Georgia
- University of Hartford
- University of Illinois
- University of Illinois at Chicago
- University of Iowa
- University of Kansas
- University of Kentucky
- University of Louisville
- University of Maine
- University of Maryland
- University of Maryland – Baltimore County
- University of Massachusetts
- University of Miami
- University of Michigan
- University of Minnesota
- University of Mississippi
- University of Missouri
- University of Montana
- University of Mount Union
- University of Nebraska
- University of Nevada – Las Vegas
- University of New Hampshire
- University of North Carolina
- University of North Carolina – Greensboro
- University of Notre Dame
- University of Oklahoma
- University of Oregon
- University of Pennsylvania
- University of Phoenix
- University of Pittsburgh
- University of Puget Sound
- University of Rhode Island
- University of Richmond
- University of Rochester
- University of San Diego
- University of San Francisco
- University of South Carolina
- University of South Dakota
- University of South Florida
- University of Southern California
- University of St Thomas – Texas
- University of Tampa
- University of Tennessee
- University of Tennessee at Chattanooga
- University of Texas
- University of Utah
- University of Vermont
- University of Virginia
- University of Washington
- University of Western Ontario
- University of Wisconsin
- University of Wisconsin – Stout
- Urbana University
- Ursinus College
- Valencia Community College
- Valparaiso University
- Vanderbilt University
- Vassar College
- Villanova University
- Virginia Commonwealth University
- Virginia Tech
- Virginia Union University
- Wagner College
- Wake Forest University
- Warren Wilson College
- Washington & Jefferson College
- Washington & Lee University
- Washington University in St. Louis
- Wellesley College
- Wesleyan University
- West Los Angeles College
- West Point Military Academy
- West Virginia University
- Western Illinois University
- Western Kentucky University
- Wheaton College (Ill.)
- Wheaton College (Mass.)
- Whitman College
- Wilkes University
- Willamette University
- Williams College
- Xavier University
- Yale University
- Youngstown State University

Order now! • collegeprowler.com • (800) 290-2682
More than 400 single-school guides available!

CPSIA information can be obtained at www.ICGtesting.com
Printed in the USA
BVOW040022250112
281250BV00003B/1/P